THE BULLEID PACIFICS OF THE SOUTHERN REGION

THE
BULLEID PACIFICS
OF THE SOUTHERN REGION

By

CECIL J. ALLEN
M.Inst.T., A.I.Loco.E.

and

S. C. TOWNROE
A.M.I.Mech.E.

WITH FOREWORD BY
O. V. S. BULLEID
C.B.E., M.I.Mech.E., M.I.Loco.E.

LONDON :
IAN ALLAN LTD

First published 1951

Reprinted 1976

All rights reserved. No part of this book may be
reproduced or transmitted in any form or by any
means, electronic or mechanical, including photo-
copying, recording or by any information storage
and retrieval system, without permission from the
Publisher in writing.

© Ian Allan Ltd, 1976

Published by Ian Allan Ltd, Shepperton, Surrey,
and printed in the United Kingdom by
Ian Allan Printing Ltd.

FOREWORD

THE enterprise of Mr. Ian Allan in publishing works on railway matters is recognised throughout the railway service and by no section so wholeheartedly as by the locomotive men. All the compilations of this firm, such as the Locomotive A.B.C. books, are so popular that they appear to borrow wings of their own by the way in which they are usually missing from the bookshelves when most needed ; their usefulness cannot be overstated.

Any new book from the same source is always welcome. " The Locomotive Exchanges," by my old friend Mr. Cecil J. Allen, was a most welcome contribution to locomotive literature. Now we have the present volume and this will, I trust, give as much pleasure to its readers as the other books published by Ian Allan Ltd.

Every locomotive designer hopes that the product of his mental turmoil and anxiety will provide his Company with a better locomotive than those presently in service, and that it will put in the hands of the operating department machines able to maintain higher average speeds with heavier loads than previously. The present book will help in forming a picture of these Southern Railway Pacifics, the last English high speed locomotives to be built by private enterprise in an atmosphere in which engineering progress had free play.

I hope that the reader, when perusing this book, may feel something of the satisfaction of the men who designed and built these engines when they see them out on the road, contributing so largely to the Southern's outstanding punctuality record.

O. V. S. BULLEID.

Coras Iompair Eireann,
Inchicore Works,
Dublin, Eire.

CONTENTS

AUTHORS' PREFACE

THIS book deals with the series of Pacific locomotives built by the Southern Railway Company under the direction of its last Chief Mechanical Engineer, Mr. O. V. S. Bulleid. During the lifetime of the " Southern," its management had shown a progressive outlook, manifested chiefly in dock and electrification schemes, the latter being accompanied by heavy expenditure upon re-signalling and rebuilding of stations ; by comparison, the money spent on new steam locomotives, especially from 1930 onwards, and upon the reconstruction of Motive Power depots, was insignificant. As if by way of atonement for this apparent neglect, however, in the closing years of the Company one hundred and forty Pacific locomotives were built to an extremely original design.

It is now ten years since the first S.R. Pacifics took the road, and a comprehensive study of these interesting locomotives is presented in this book for the benefit of locomotive enthusiasts. An encouraging sign of the times is an increased demand, by those who take a keen interest in railway matters, for information of a more technical character than has been generally available in the past. The joint authors have endeavoured to meet the request for an explanation of the principal features of the Bulleid Pacifics in a manner neither superficial nor yet abstruse. Where originality is displayed there will always be controversy, and the authors, in the full knowledge that opinion may be based on a particular point of view, do not claim the competence to adjudicate in such matters. Any preference expressed for one feature as against another, however, must be regarded as that of the authors unless otherwise stated, and not necessarily as that of the members of the Railway Executive responsible for locomotive design.

There is a great deal of truth in the saying that the man who never makes a mistake never achieves anything ; it applies in all walks of life, locomotive engineering included. Science keeps moving onward, and the designer who is content to follow a tradition, even when it is sound, will find that tradition followed too slavishly leads to stagnation. Courage is needed when venturing into unexplored fields of development, and Mr. O. V. S. Bulleid's pioneering work has made a notable contribution to the sum of knowledge in the field of locomotive engineering.

In presenting this book, the authors are much indebted to Mr. Bulleid for his kindly foreword, and also make their grateful acknowledgments of the assistance received from numerous friends and colleagues, and to various sources of published information, including the designer's paper " ' Merchant Navy ' Class Locomotives of the Southern Railway " read before the Institution of Mechanical Engineers. In dealing with Pacific performance, the first of the two undersigned, who was responsible personally for timing many of the runs described, has followed his usual custom of writing in the first person singular, as this adds life to an enthralling story.

CECIL J. ALLEN.
STEPHEN C. TOWNROE.

CHAPTER ONE

THE CONDITIONS TO BE FACED

F ROM 1926 until the outbreak of the Second World War the largest express passenger locomotive class on the Southern Railway was the " Lord Nelson " 4-6-0, which had been designed by Mr. R. E. L. Maunsell to deal with trains of 500 tons in weight at average speeds of 55 m.p.h. When Mr. O. V. S. Bulleid, who had previously been Sir Nigel Gresley's assistant on the L.N.E.R., in 1938 succeeded Mr. R. E. L. Maunsell as Chief Mechanical Engineer of the Southern Railway, the future " target " figures for express passenger trains had risen to 550-600 tons in weight, and to speeds of 60 m.p.h. average on the Eastern Section and 70 m.p.h. average on the Western Section. The " Lord Nelson " class, with a tractive effort of 33,488 lb., in power was by then a long way behind the latest productions of the other railway companies.

In 1933 a Southern Pacific design had been proposed and discussed with the Civil Engineer, and for several years afterwards the subject was revived from time to time, but for various reasons it did not reach a conclusive stage. The first Pacific projected was, in effect, an enlarged " Lord Nelson " with 6 ft. 3 in. driving wheels like those of No. 859. The need for such an engine was based mainly on the demands of the Eastern Section boat trains, but any design capable of putting up a good performance on that Section of the Southern Railway certainly would not find any other route a stiffer proposition.

To secure any improvements in the timings of the Dover and Folkestone boat trains without exceeding reasonable maximum speeds on the level stretches, it was clear that higher speeds would have to be maintained uphill. Smarter get-aways would have to be made from the starting stations and the locomotives must be capable of accelerating the trains rapidly from speed restriction points and from the signal checks which were not always avoidable in the densely-occupied electrified suburban area, where the speed of steam trains was limited by that of the electrics. With the progress of electrification during the Southern Railway *regime*, electric and steam trains were treading more and more on one another's heels, and approximately one-third of the mileage to Dover was by now electrified. Furthermore, the sleeping-car trains running between London and Paris by way of the Dover-Dunkerque train ferry just prior to the war were too heavy for one engine and had to be double-headed.

The emphasis on a larger boiler and firebox in Mr. Maunsell's proposed Pacific was significant. To produce better accelerative characteristics in any design, the obvious theory is to " gear the engine down " by providing small driving wheels. This theory has often been upset. The G.W.R. " Castles," for instance, have displayed superlative powers of acceleration and hill-climbing and yet their driving wheels, 6 ft. 8½ in. in diameter, are comparatively large. " Lord Nelson " 4-6-0 No. 859 *Lord Hood*, fitted with 6 ft. 3 in. driving wheels instead of 6 ft. 7 in., had shown no inclination to excel the other engines of the same class in performance, and similar examples could be quoted. The fact is that the acceleration depends mainly upon the way in which the locomotive is handled. No driver will urge his engine to a vigorous start if, by doing so, he draws too heavily upon the reserves of steam and water in his boiler, and tears the fire to pieces in the process. He will not charge up gradients " all out " if this results in a loss of 30 lb. or so of steam pressure by the time he reaches the summit, leaving him in difficulties for a faster, level section. He certainly will not turn the top of a bank on to a downhill section with low water showing in the gauge glasses, for the change of gradient affects the water level in the boiler, and may result in the firebox crown becoming uncovered if the level has fallen too low.

The " Lord Nelsons " steamed well, but their boilers did not possess the reserves needed for any heavier handling by the engine crews. Mr. Maunsell intended to provide his Pacific with a boiler carrying the same pressure as the " Lord Nelsons," 220 lb., but with larger water capacity and with an enlarged, wide firebox having a grate area of 40 sq. ft., easier to fire than the long, narrow " Nelson " firebox.

When the success of the " Schools " class became evident, the trend of thought at Waterloo inclined towards three cylinders instead of four, and as *Lord Hood* had not proved a noticeably better performer with 6 ft. 3 in. diameter driving wheels, the next proposal was for a Pacific with three 20 in. by 28 in. cylinders, 6 ft. 7 in. coupled wheels, and 220 lb. boiler pressure, capable of about 1,700 drawbar horsepower. The estimated weight proved too heavy for acceptance by the Civil Engineer, but a modified version of the design, with 19 in. cylinders and capable of 1,500 drawbar horsepower, was virtually accepted, although the routes over which it could be permitted were so few that the justification for building a new class was almost nullified. To secure greater route availability, the 2-6-2 type was next considered, in the form of an enlarged Maunsell three-cylinder 2-6-0 of the " U1 " class.

At this stage Mr. Maunsell suffered a breakdown in health, and during the last years of his term of office activity in new design work was in a state of suspension. In the meantime, the Civil Engineer was making steady progress with his strengthening of bridges and permanent way, and when Mr. O. V. S. Bulleid took over, in 1937, the revival of the Pacific design met with more favour than previously. Mr. Bulleid had been closely associated with the successful L.N.E.R. Pacifics and with their high-speed performances ; he also had a wide knowledge of foreign locomotive design. His first Pacific design for the Southern, the " Merchant Navy " class, incorporated a really adequate boiler and followed contemporary French practice, in which were incorporated boilers with 284 lb. pressure and all-welded steel fireboxes with thermic syphons.

In his new design Mr. Bulleid produced a boiler that could really " take it "—or should one say " give it " ? With 280 lb. pressure, not only was the potential power increased, but the increase of 60 lb. over a 220 lb. boiler gave, in effect, 60 lb. in reserve if one assumes, as in fact is often the case, that 220 lb. is adequate to meet the maximum demands on the more level stretches of road. The net result is to give the driver the confidence that plenty of steam is available when required, and the outstanding performances of the Bulleid Pacifics during the 1948 Interchange Trials, particularly in acceleration and hill-climbing, were the proof of the pudding. In fact, so ample is the boiler capacity of the " Merchant Navy " class that there is every indication that the engines could be worked persistently at higher rates of output than could reasonably be sustained by hand-firing, and it was for this reason that a Berkley mechanical stoker was fitted, for trial purposes, to " Merchant Navy " 4-6-2 No. 35005 *Canadian Pacific*. The stoker had the advantage that it could deal also with low grade, dusty coal, but it involved the selection of small coal, less in size than 6 in. cubes, which the ordinary coaling plants at the sheds could not grade for the purpose. Had sufficient engines of this type been fitted with mechanical stokers, the cost of modifying coaling plants to supply this type of fuel separately would have merited consideration, but in the circumstances, although the stoker worked quite efficiently, it was decided to remove the equipment from the engine.

But we are getting too far ahead with the story. It is one thing to conceive a powerful Pacific with a big boiler, and quite another thing to build it within the limits of weight, height, length and width laid down by the Civil Engineer. The limits which circumscribed the designer of the " Merchant Navy " class were very severe, and particularly the principal dimensions dictated by the loading gauge of the S.R. Eastern Section, which were as follows :

Maximum height of engine above rail (on centre-line)	13 ft.	1 in.
,, width over cab	9 ft.	0 in.
,, height of cab cornice above rail	10 ft.	11 in.
,, width over cylinders	8 ft.	10 in.

The L.N.E.R. and L.M.S.R. Pacifics and the G.W.R. " Kings " and " Castles " all exceed these limits in one dimension or another.

CHAPTER TWO

THE "MERCHANT NAVY" CLASS

T HE problem that faced Mr. Bulleid, in the design of an engine which would have the tractive effort and the boiler capacity to meet new conditions of traffic, without exceeding the main line axle-load of 21 tons, and restricted by the Southern Railway composite loading gauge, was eventually solved by a bold and original approach. In his attack on the problem, Mr. Bulleid took advantage of the tremendous strides made by the electric welding process to design an engine in which heavy castings, with a few exceptions, were replaced by fabricated parts, that is to say, parts constructed of pieces of steel plate cut to shape and joined by welding. Welding was used wherever possible instead of riveting. The whole structure of a locomotive was conceived anew, from scratch, with the object of keeping down the weight to a minimum.

The wheel-splashers, running boards and heavy plates used in the conventional superstructure were abandoned and, instead, the upper portion of the locomotive was covered with a light plate casing, the shape of which was governed by the Belpaire-top firebox. The casing plates were carried on channel-section ribs, attached to the main frames. The smokebox was made the same shape as the casing, and it also conformed to the set of the main steam pipes inside the smokebox, a more logical arrangement than the ordinary circular smokebox. The chimney, far from being a heavy ornamental casting, was made of thin steel plate, and for its support required only a light plate roof to the smokebox. So light, in fact, that observers from above have noticed these flat smokebox tops pulsating with the blast when the engines are working hard! Weight-saving by the use of light steel plate, joined by electric welding instead of riveting, was pursued in every detail, from the front of the engine to the rear of the tender. Considerations of cost and availability alone prevented the extended use of light alloys in the design. The shape of the tender conformed to that of modern coaching stock, so that the *ensemble* was " air-smoothed," a description more correct than " streamlined " in its proper sense.

A boiler pressure of 280 lb. was in advance of anything previously in use in the British Isles, apart from one or two experimental locomotives. For such a pressure, and corresponding temperature, copper was not considered to be desirable for the construction of the firebox, and progressive increases in boiler pressure with copper fireboxes were known to result in increased maintenance troubles and more frequent firebox renewals at general repairs. Steel is used to-day all over the world for locomotive fireboxes ; indeed, locomotives on the North American Continent use nothing else, and the quality of steel plate suitable for the manufacture of fireboxes has improved considerably since the early

12

trials of this metal, which prejudiced British engineers against it. Steel plate can be welded easily by the electric arc, and the construction of a firebox by welding eliminates the troublesome riveted lap joints employed in copper construction ; moreover, during repairs, defective portions of the firebox can be cut out by oxy-acetylene flame and new portions welded in as required.

A reduction in weight of some 30 cwt. in the firebox alone was secured by the use of steel ; the thickness of plate used was ⅜-inch. All boiler welds were subjected to X-ray examination during manufacture. The boiler tubes also were sealed by welding at the firebox tubeplate. Credit is due both to Mr. Bulleid, who pioneered this extensive use of welding in British locomotive boilers, and also to the North British Locomotive Company, which made the first ten of these boilers.

Two thermic syphons were fitted in the firebox, connected from the lower part of the tubeplate to the crown. These provide additional rigidity to the firebox and support the crown sheet, forming an additional safeguard against any collapse of the crown sheet that might result from low water ; in addition, six fusible plugs in the crown afford ample protection in less serious cases of low water. The brick arch is in three sections ; there is a centre section between the syphons, flanked by outer sections between the syphons and the firebox sides. The syphons provide additional and valuable heating surface in the hottest part of the firebox, and they also stimulate circulation, as they provide a natural path for convection currents.

The boiler barrel was designed to be horizontal on the top, to give maximum steam space, and was tapered underneath. This taper enabled the floor of the smokebox to be high enough to clear the inside cylinder, with its valve above it, besides assisting the flow of water, by gravity, towards the firebox from the front ring of the barrel, where the feed water was introduced through the clackboxes. The regulator was of the circular valve pattern, taking steam from beneath a shallow dome without a steam collector pipe.

Three " pop " safety-valves were fitted on the front ring of the barrel, an unusual position. The usual firebox location for safety-valves was avoided in view of the possibility of lifting water as well as steam from the turbulent area over a firebox fitted with thermic syphons. In their present position, however, surging of the boiler water during heavy braking is apt to cause the valves to lift at below the maximum pressure at which they are set, so that in avoiding one trouble another has been incurred.

In designing the very original valve-gear, several aims and objectives were borne in mind. Consideration was first given to the possibility of a valve-motion which could be contained in easily-interchangeable boxes, after the style of certain proprietary poppet valve-gears but without necessarily employing poppet-valves. This idea had obvious advantages, but its realisation was so difficult of attainment that the alternative was adopted of total enclosure of the valve-motion, in order to obtain as much freedom from dirt and wear as that enjoyed by the working parts of an internal-combustion engine.

Such an arrangement promised not only reduced maintenance but also a reduction in number of the many oiling points that require the attention of a driver during preparation of a locomotive of traditional design. At least one modern express locomotive type has over ninety oiling points, including some on the inside motion which are very awkwardly located, so that a driver of stoutish build can hardly be blamed if he allocates their care and attention to his mate. It is even said that one driver caused a late start to his train by becoming firmly wedged in the motion of his engine ! Furthermore, the high speeds and long non-stop runs involved in working such trains as the pre-war " Coronation " and " Coronation Scot " were known to have shown up some weaknesses in the traditional methods of lubrication (by trimmings and independent oilboxes on each working part) so that the adoption of flood lubrication, in an oil-bath, offered greater security from heated bearings at any higher speeds that might be demanded in the future.

The arrangement of the Bulleid-Walschaerts gear can be followed with the aid of the photograph on page 20, which shows a demonstration model of one set of valve-gear. The outside return cranks and inside eccentrics, which transmit their movement to the expansion links in the conventional Walschaerts layout, were replaced by a chain-driven three-throw crankshaft, in between the frames, performing the same function of actuating the expansion links. When this fundamental difference is grasped by the amateur, the mystery of this valve-motion disappears. To enable three sets of valve-gear, one for each of the three cylinders, to fit neatly into the space between the frames, the full throw of the expansion links was made less than that required to give full travel to the valves, and the movement was amplified by making the rocker arms of unequal length, in the proportion of 3 to 8. In other words, $1\frac{1}{2}$ inches of movement in the radius rod give 4 inches travel to the valve.

The inside connecting rod, crank-axle, big-end, little-end, inside crosshead and slide-bars, together with the three sets of valve motion, are contained within a sump holding 40 gallons of oil. Two gear pumps, driven by a chain off the three-throw crankshaft, deliver oil over these parts by means of perforated pipes. The pressure of oil is indicated on the footplate by two gauges, one for each pump, and the oil pressure is about 15-20 lb. when running.

The three-throw crankshaft is driven by inverted-tooth chains ; the chain connected to the crank-axle is horizontal, and allows for a rise and fall of the crank-axle on its springs. This chain runs to the intermediate sprocket and a second chain connects with the three-throw crankshaft, low down in the sump. For adjustment of the chain tension, during repairs, the intermediate sprocket cradle is made adjustable. The three-throw crankshaft revolves at the same speed, of course, as the crank axle, and each crank on the shaft is in phase with the appropriate big-end. Incidentally, the weight imposed by the sprocket and a proportion of the chain on the driving axle adds little to the unsprung weight on that axle.

Three cylinders, 18 inches diameter by 24 inches stroke, were adopted ; the two outside cylinders are slightly inclined at 1 in 40, and the inside cylinder at 1 in $7\frac{3}{4}$. To permit the steam passages from the valves to the cylinders to be as straight as possible, outside admission valves were employed ; the valve-gear was arranged as for inside admission and the rocker arms reverse the movements. Each valve is driven by an arm in the exhaust cavity, thus avoiding the use of external valve-spindles under pressure of live steam. A shaft passes transversely through each cylinder casting to connect the driven and driving arms. All these parts are between the frames and cannot be seen from the outside of the engine. The exhaust passages from the outside cylinders were connected to the inside exhaust passage by large-section pipes. Over the inside exhaust cavity was mounted the short multiple-jet blast pipe, having five jets, each $2\frac{5}{8}$ inches diameter.

A hydrostatic lubricator on the footplate, and two mechanical lubricators in front of the smokebox, were fitted to the first ten " Merchant Navy " Pacifics ; all later Pacifics, however, have been equipped with three mechanical lubricators in front of the smokebox. One lubricator provides oil, through atomisers, to the valves and pistons, while the other two provide lubrication for the rocker shafts. On some of the engines one central oil reservoir has been fitted to supply all three lubricators. The drive to these lubricators is taken from the valve-gear, and the amount of oil delivered varies with the cut-off.

The coupled-wheel diameter adopted was 6 feet 2 inches, so that the engines should have a versatile, mixed-traffic character ; and to keep down the piston-speed at high revolutions of the driving wheels, the piston-stroke was made the comparatively short one of 24 inches. Another interesting point about the design was the closer-than-normal spacing of the frames, whereby the centres of the horn-cheeks were brought into line with the frames. Greater rigidity in the horns lessens the risk of frame fractures, since the apertures cut in the frame for the horns and axle-boxes are a potential source of frame weakness.

The unusual brake-gear involved the use of two brake-blocks on each coupled wheel, arranged in clasp fashion, thus not only ensuring a generous area of brake-block surface in contact with the tyre, but also avoiding the displacement of the axlebox which must occur when a brake-block is applied on one side of a wheel only. Although the latter arrangement is common enough, it may be a contributory cause, occasionally, of heated bearings. The restriction upon the coupled wheelbase, and so upon the space between any two coupled wheels, however, prevented the use of brake-blocks fixed on the horizontal centre-line, and the force of single brake-blocks applied upon the lower segment of a wheel must tend to pull an engine down on its springs, by virtue of the upward component of the force applied to the wheel. A steam cylinder operates the engine brakes and a vacuum cylinder the tender brakes ; insufficient space was available for vacuum cylinders on the engine, and economy in weight was possible with steam rather than vacuum brake apparatus.

The disc wheel centres, known as the " B.F.B." (Bulleid-Firth-Brown) type, are 10 per cent lighter than spoked wheels, and stronger ; hence they provide more uniform support to the tyre than spokes, and reduce the incidence of loose tyres. These wheel centres were made of cast steel, but one experimental set of wheel centres has been fabricated. The bogie design was similar to the satisfactory " Lord Nelson " design, but the trailing truck was original, in employing three-point suspension, with sliding pads and spring side-control underneath the footplate. To enginemen used to the rather harsh riding of a 4-6-0 locomotive, the effect of a pony truck under the footplate end was something of a revelation ; by comparison with the 4-6-0s, the Bulleid Pacifics give an " armchair ride," even when due for overhaul.

Another special feature of the design was that no over-balance for the reciprocating parts was added in the coupled wheels to the balance weights for the revolving parts. The result was to eliminate hammer-blow on the rail. This complete absence of hammer-blow was demonstrated, to the satisfaction of the Civil Engineer, by observations of the deflections of a bridge over which a " Merchant Navy " class engine made a series of high-speed runs, and this feature alone rendered the design a most acceptable one to the bridge experts. Theoretically, the absence of any reciprocating balance leaves certain secondary unbalanced forces free to affect the motion of the engine, in the form of side-thrusts, but in practice no disturbance is felt on the footplate of the Bulleid Pacifics for this reason.

CHAPTER THREE

THE BULLEID CAB

THE foregoing chapter has given the reader an idea of the remarkable originality displayed in the design of the first Southern Pacific. Credit was added to the achievement in the fact that the locomotives were at the drawing board stage on the outbreak of war, and yet, in spite of many difficulties and distractions, the first Pacific was ready for trials early in 1941.

Many other features of the design call for some mention here. The cab, for instance, gave a better standard of comfort and protection for the engine crew than almost any other British locomotive then running, and only in the hottest weather does the modern driver yearn for the old fresh-air style of accommodation provided by locomotive engineers of the Nineteenth Century ! Electric lighting was installed, with headlamps at front and rear, lights under the casing over the wheels and lights in the cab, and independent lighting fittings for the reverser, water gauges, and injectors, all supplied with current from a small steam-driven generator set.

The layout of the footplate controls was arranged so that the fittings in frequent use by the driver were placed on the left-hand or driving side, and those used by the fireman on the right-hand side. One of the drawbacks of standardisation in the past has been evident in the repetition of a standard footplate arrangement on new engines year after year. For example, it has been customary for a long time to fit one injector on the driver's side and the other on the fireman's side, presumably because this permits a symmetrical arrangement of the water feeds and steam cocks. Mr. Bulleid's policy was to fit two injectors on the fireman's side where either injector, or both, could be worked without disturbing the driver. With the injectors on separate sides, there is a risk that the driver's side injector will be so little used that when it is required in a hurry it is found to be unworkable. Mr. Bulleid also introduced the steam-operated firedoor to British practice. The fireman can open the firehole doors by pressing a pedal on the footplate.

The size of the firebox left little room for the cab front windows on the original design, and the absence of running boards, and the forward position of the windows, made it difficult to clean them. Larger windows have since been obtained by the V-front pattern cab, in which they are set within arm's length of the sliding side windows to make cleaning a simple matter.

The whistle deserves mention : the note was chosen as a nice compromise between the offensive shriek of a high-pitched whistle and the bassoon tone of the Caledonian hooter adopted by the L.M.S.R. The note approximates to middle C, although the initial

16

Navy No. 35025 (unnamed at the time) approaches Clapham Junction with the 3.20 p.m. Waterloo-Bournemouth express on July 9th, 1949. [C. C. B. Herbert

17

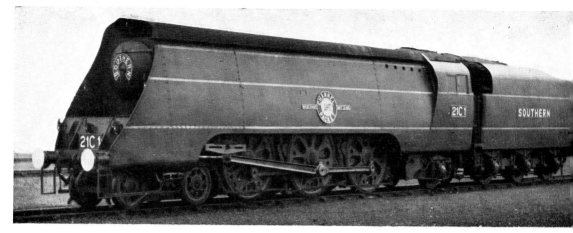

IN ORIGINAL FORM—" Merchant Navy " No. 21C1 *Channel Packet* as built. *British Railways*

DESIGNER—Mr. O. V. S. Bulleid (facing the camera). [*S. C. Townroe*

WARTIME BLACK LIVERY—" Merchant Navy " No. 21C9 *Shaw Savill*. [*British Railways*

THE SECOND SERIES—"Merchant Navy" No. 21C17 *Belgian Marine*, with modified front end, cab and tender.   [*British Railways*

WITH MODIFIED CAB—Following the introduction of the "Battle of Britain" light Pacific, "Merchant Navy" No. 21C8 *Orient Line* was modified with a similar type of cab. Photographed at Eastleigh on August 29th, 1947.   [*L. Elsey*

THE THIRD SERIES—"Merchant Navy" No. 35029, with nameplates boarded over, as was the custom prior to naming ceremonies. Note 6,000 gallon tender and new cab design, now the standard for most "Merchant Navies."   [*P. Ransome-Wallis*

Above : UNDER CONSTRUCTION—A " West Country " Pacific at Brighton Works. [*C. R. L. Coles*

Below : THE BULLEID-WALSCHAERTS VALVE GEAR—Photograph of a model showing the arrangement for one cylinder.

[*British Railways*

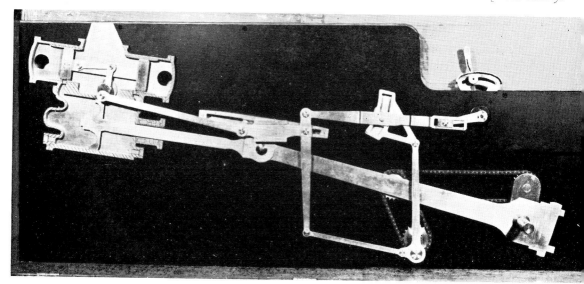

FIRST ASSIGNMENT—The "Merchant Navies" began their life on the West of England main line. No. 21C1 *Channel Packet* pulls out of Exeter Central (*above*) with an up express on August 26th, 1946.   The up "Atlantic Coast Express," photographed near Pirbright (*below*), is headed by No. 21C11 *General Steam Navigation*.   [*B. A. Butt, C. J. Grose*

MIXED TRAFFIC—In their early wartime days, the " Merchant Navies " tackled quite an amount of freight traffic ; in this picture (*above*) No. 21C7 *Aberdeen Commonwealth* is in charge of an up milk empties train near West Weybridge. No. 35006 *Peninsular & Oriental S.N. Co.* finds itself with no more than three coaches to play with (*below*), forming a relief train from Waterloo to the West on April 16th, 1949, and photographed near Surbiton.

[*E. R. Wethersett, C. C. B. Herbert*

ON THE EASTERN SECTION—The first
regular operation of a "Merchant Navy" to
the Kent coast was by No. 21C7 *Aberdeen
Commonwealth*, which worked between London
and Ramsgate for a week in October, 1944.
The engine is seen (*above*) at Herne Bay on
its first appearance there, October 11th, 1944.
No. 21C1 was used for the first post-war run
of the "Golden Arrow" (*below*) on April 13th,
1946, and carried the special emblem on the
side of the casing (*right*). "Merchant Navies"
did not re-appear on the Eastern Section until
the close of 1949.

[*P. Ransome-Wallis, British Railways,
Rev. A. C. Cawston*

SPECIAL OCCASIONS—" Strangers " are sometimes drafted to the Eastern Section to handle special trains for " V.I.Ps." " Merchant Navy " No. 35004 *Cunard White Star* leaves Dover on November 21st, 1950, with the Pullman special conveying the Queen of the Netherlands to London. On June 1st, 1950, " Merchant Navy " No. 35019 *French Line CGT* (*below*) achieved a S.R. record by running a royal special between Waterloo and Sherborne, 118.3 miles, non-stop in both directions. [*P. Ransome-Wallis, J. B. Heyman*

condensation in the horizontally-mounted whistle sometimes causes a little hesitancy in its utterance !

The tender was fabricated from steel plate $\frac{3}{16}$ in. thick. It is fitted with a cab, containing the tool and clothing cupboards and with coal doors to prevent, as far as possible, the entry of coal dust. Coal watering pipes were provided in the coal bunker, operated from a cock on one injector. Windows were built into the tender front for use when running tender first, and two filling holes were provided in the cab, in addition to the manhole in the back of the tender, intended for greater convenience in filling. To provide against possible water shortage on the longer runs, especially between Waterloo and Bournemouth (in view of the absence of water-troughs), some of the engines have been fitted with a larger tender with a 6,000-gallon tank—the biggest tender tank in Great Britain.

A modified Continental system of numbering was used, to identify the type of engine by the prefix (21C), but the system did not prove popular, partly because it was more cumbersome, and partly because, in spite of many different classes of locomotive in use on the Southern, numbers and classes could easily be identified by those concerned with everyday working of the engines. The number of engines working in a particular district is limited and numerals in three figures are usually significant enough for local use, though comprehensive numbering systems are necessary, of course, to identify engines at central administrative and statistical offices. The " 21C " system remained in use for " Merchant Navy " and, later, the " West Country " class engines, until Nationalisation.

The original " Merchant Navy " engines carried the letters and numbers on the cab sides and in front of the engine, on cast gunmetal plates. An ornamental circular plate bearing the name " Southern," with " Eastleigh " and the date of construction, was fitted to the smokebox door. These plates were not continued on all the engines, and have since been removed as the engines have come in for general repairs.

The names of the first Pacifics were chosen to mark the long association that the Southern Railway, and its predecessors, had with shipping companies. It will be remembered that the London & South Western Railway purchased the docks at Southampton in 1892 from the original Dock Company, and proceeded to develop the port for ocean-going traffic. This development work was carried on by the Southern Railway, with the building of the new docks and the King George V Graving Dock, and the facilities which the port of Southampton now offers to the world's largest liners are the result of railway enterprise under private ownership. The London, Brighton & South Coast and South Eastern & Chatham Companies also had developed their Continental services, and smaller ports on Southern territory had been connected with coastal shipping. Moreover, the title for the new locomotive class was chosen at a time when the Merchant Navy was playing a critical part in the drama of the Second World War. The name plaques bear the house flag of each shipping company, and these plaques are right- and left-handed, so that the flag flies the right way on each side of the engine for the normal direction of travel. The names, present numbers and building dates of the " Merchant Navy " Pacifics, all of which have been built at Eastleigh, are set out in Appendix B.

CHAPTER FOUR

The First Pacifics In Service

THE first " Merchant Navy " Pacific was completed at Eastleigh Works in February, 1941 : on February 22nd a trial train of twenty coaches was hauled from Eastleigh to Bournemouth and back. The engine was named *Channel Packet* on March 10th, 1941, at a ceremony held at Eastleigh.

By that date, boat train traffic on the Eastern Division had ceased entirely, and trains in that part of England were being involved in some rather unsporting contests with enemy aircraft ; incidentally, a " Merchant Navy " 4-6-2 No. 21C4 *Cunard White Star* (now No. 35004) was destined to be shot up by a German raider in November, 1942, near Whimple, but fortunately without serious injury to the engine crew. The main line to the West of England, however, was carrying heavy wartime traffic. West of Salisbury the main line trains, loaded to capacity, were making additional stops, and the stalwart " King Arthurs " were having a hard time of it, especially where the stopping stations were awkwardly placed in relation to the gradients.

It was therefore decided to use the new engines on the Western Division. To permit time to be kept, the agreed maximum load for " King Arthur " 4-6-0s between Salisbury and Exeter was 11 bogies, or 355 tons, though before the outbreak of war, in exceptional circumstances, some amazing feats of timekeeping had been achieved by " King Arthurs " with twelve or thirteen bogies. Eventually it was shown that the " Merchant Navy " engines could handle up to 16 bogies with ease, and, on occasion, even 17 or 18, without assistance over the exceedingly steep gradients of this route, so that the " King Arthurs," after a long supremacy, at last had found their superiors. Other new engines had been defeated on this ground in the past ; Drummond's four-cylinder 4-6-0s with 6 ft. wheels, for example, had failed to distinguish themselves, and Maunsell's " Lord Nelsons " never took kindly to the Exeter road. The Bulleid Pacifics, on the contrary, soon began to show a complete mastery.

The engines were not without their teething troubles, however, and for this reason a good deal of the earliest running had to be on freight trains. One cannot break away from old, well-proven features of design in engineering without such troubles, and they only show how much remains to be discovered about the behaviour of metals under stress and the magnitude of the stresses which occur in the parts of a locomotive at work. Even now it is not possible to claim that the design is as trouble-free as conventional designs which have undergone years of painstaking improvements to reduce all known causes of failure. On the other hand, it was felt in many quarters that locomotive design had fallen into a rut. There were signs of creeping paralysis in drawing offices once famed for a progressive outlook. The diesels were knocking on the tomb of George Stephenson, to the accompaniment of loud humming from the electrical fraternity, and something ought to be done about it !

The " Merchant Navy " class boiler has undoubtedly proved successful as a steam producer and the maintenance compares favourably with boilers of the usual construction. Electric welding equipment and trained welders are now available at the running sheds, to give prompt attention to any necessary boiler repairs. The direct arrangement of steampipes, ample port area, and outside admission valves, have been found to give a very free running engine, capable of high speeds, as is fully demonstrated in Chapters 6 to 10 of this book. Though no high speed tests have been carried out similar to those conducted on the L.M.S.R. and L.N.E.R. in 1935, 1937 and 1938, a speed of 98 m.p.h. has been reached on nearly level track between Tonbridge and Ashford, on a test run, and there is no doubt that maximum speeds of over 100 m.p.h. could be attained by Southern Pacifics should exceptionally fast travel be desired.

The total enclosure of the motion was, perforce, carried out by building the oil bath in the frame structure of the engine ; thus it does not strictly compare with the crankcase of an internal combustion engine, which is a separate unit and is usually fixed on anti-vibration mountings. Considerable flexure of a locomotive takes place while it is running, which makes it difficult to maintain oil tightness with the " Merchant Navy " design, and accounts for very heavy consumption of lubricant. The crank-axle has to pass through the sump, and has to rise and fall, although oil deflectors are fitted on the axle adjacent to the inside faces of the axle-boxes. Defects in working parts on an ordinary locomotive can easily be seen, very often in time to prevent failure on the road, but with the enclosure of the motion this is not the case, and once an engine has shown signs of trouble, the driver may have difficulty in diagnosing the defect and may have to give up his engine as a total failure. These matters are dealt with in greater detail in Chapter 11.

In December, 1944, various modifications were made to the design and the second ten engines, Nos. 21C11 to 21C20, now Nos. 35011 to 35020, began to take the road. They were all allocated to Nine Elms Depot. Ever since " King Arthur " class No. 777 *Sir Lamiel* covered the 83¾ miles from Salisbury to Waterloo in 72¼ minutes, Nine Elms drivers have had ambitions to make the run in 72 minutes or less, and the " Merchant Navy " engines were soon seen to be the very thing for the task ! It is the driver's dream that on the last day of work before he retires, he will have a good engine, a fireman named Hercules, and every signal off from Waterloo to Salisbury ! Joking apart, a timing of this kind has now become a practical possibility.

In the autumn of 1948, a further ten engines of the class, Nos. 35021 to 35030, were put under construction at Eastleigh Works, and of these the first four, Nos. 35021 to 35024, were allocated to Exmouth Junction and the remainder, Nos. 35025 to 35030, to Bournemouth. The first appearance of a " Merchant Navy " 4-6-2 on the Eastern section had been in October, 1944, when No. 21C7 *Aberdeen Commonwealth* worked the 8.55 a.m. from Victoria to Ramsgate. Later, in August, 1945, No. 21C2 *Union Castle* made some test runs between Victoria and Dover, and in October, 1945, No. 21C17 *Belgian Marine* worked the Ostend boat train from Victoria to Dover, after a naming ceremony at Victoria. In April, 1946, No. 21C1 *Channel Packet* was used for a special run from London to Dover with guests and representatives of the Press, to celebrate the restoration of the

" Golden Arrow " service. In 1950 the six Bournemouth " Merchant Navy " Pacifics were transferred to the Eastern Division for the heaviest boat train workings, the Night Ferry in particular, which had got beyond the capacity of the smaller Pacifics.

During the career of the " Merchant Navy " Pacifics on the Western Division, the schedules of the main line passenger trains have remained, for the most part, on the moderate speed basis to which they were eased during the war, and not until 1949 and 1950 were the first post-war accelerations made. So the engines have not had to face any daily task calling for the maintenance of full boiler pressure throughout the journey, and in this respect there has been a noticeable difference in the way the engines have been handled, as compared with older types with which full boiler pressure has been essential. This is clearly seen in the subsequent chapters on performance, which contain footplate observations on some typical journeys.

In 1947, the " Devon Belle " all-Pullman train was put in service between Waterloo, Plymouth and Ilfracombe, running five days in each week during the summer period. At the busiest summer week-ends this train has loaded regularly to 14 Pullmans, of some 575 tons gross weight, and has imposed the heaviest task yet set for the " Merchant Navy " Pacifics, but the engines have proved themselves more than equal to it. The train is booked to run each way between Waterloo and Sidmouth Junction with a stop at Wilton only, for locomotive-changing purposes. The initial down and up journeys of the " Devon Belle " took place on June 20th, 1947, engine No. 21C15 *Rotterdam Lloyd*, from Nine Elms, working the down and up trains between Waterloo and Wilton, while Nos. 21C3 *Royal Mail* and 21C4 *Cunard White Star*, both from Exmouth Junction, hauled the trains from Wilton to Exeter Central and in the reverse direction respectively.

CHAPTER FIVE

The "Lightweights"

FROM the point of view of engine restrictions, a railway can be divided into primary routes, secondary routes, and branch lines. The primary routes are those which carry the heaviest main line traffic and upon which expenditure has been incurred, throughout the years, in maintaining the permanent way in a fit state to carry the largest and heaviest locomotives at high speeds. From time to time the bridges have been strengthened or renewed to carry increased axle-loads and sharp curves have been eased, sometimes at the cost of acquiring additional land for the purpose. Some lines were planned as primary routes when they were constructed; others have been brought up to primary standards in order to afford alternative main line routes.

Secondary routes were often planned as " feeders " to the main lines and were not expected to carry heavy traffic. In a few cases, such as the Swanley-Ashford line, for example, costly improvements were justified, to carry boat trains. The old S.R. direct route to Dorchester and Weymouth *via* Ringwood and West Moors, however, remained a secondary route, although in an emergency, or during the summer season, it could afford a valuable alternative route to the busy Bournemouth main line *via* Sway. The whole of the Southern Railway west of Exeter had remained in the secondary, or lesser, category, mainly because the principal trains are sub-divided at Exeter and beyond, and the loads are heavy for a few months in the year only.

Considerable use is made of the secondary routes for excursions, empty stock trains, and special traffic of all kinds involving " main line " train loads often beyond the normal capacity of a Maunsell Mogul. An improvement in power thus was needed upon the " U1 " and " N " class 2-6-0s, which were the most powerful engines permitted to run west of Exeter prior to the Second World War. With a heavy excursion train routed partly over a main line and partly over a secondary line, the choice was either of changing engines on the journey or working, say, a " U " class engine throughout, with some difficulty in timekeeping over the faster and busier main line portions of the journey. The " West Country " 4-6-2 class was therefore produced with the object of providing the Motive Power Department with a " secondary route " engine which could run practically anywhere, saving only the minor branch lines.

The light Pacifics were designed as a smaller edition of the " Merchant Navy " class, and the engines became known familiarly as the " Lightweights." The principal differences in dimensions may be compared by referring to the table of Appendix A on Page 76. A slightly smaller boiler was fitted, working at the same pressure of 280 lbs., but with less

29

superheat, and mated to cylinders of 16⅜ in. diameter. The axle weights on the coupled wheels worked out at 18 tons 15 cwt. each, bringing the engine down to the Civil Engineer's requirements for secondary routes subject to special speed restrictions at certain points, and to restrictions of entry into wayside sidings of sharp curvature, on account of the long Pacific wheelbase. A programme of turntable renewals, increasing them to 70 ft. in diameter, has been put in hand to accommodate these engines.

The width of the original light Pacifics was 8 ft. 6 in. Other minor differences included the fitting of tenders with 4,500 gallons of water, as compared with the 5,000-gallon tenders of the larger engines, and the provision of open ashpans without dampers as in American practice.

The title " West Country " class was an appropriate choice, in view of the decision to devote the new engines to the needs of the traffic west of Exeter as a matter of priority, and places in the West Country were chosen for the individual names to be borne by the engines. Originally, names were proposed to cover fifty engines. At a later stage, when the requirements of the West of England had been satisfied and the number of engines available was sufficient to supply the needs of other depots, such as those on the Eastern Division, it was decided to begin a new series from No. 34048 onwards, known as the " Battle of Britain " class, with names commemorating the defeat of Hitler's " Luftwaffe " over the south-eastern counties of England.

The design of the engines continued unchanged up to No. 34070, when it was felt that it was no longer necessary to restrict the width of the engines to permit them to pass over the Tonbridge-Hastings line, which has the tightest loading gauge route included in the Southern Region " secondary " list. After No. 34070, therefore, " Battle of Britain " class engines have been built with cabs 9 ft. wide instead of 8 ft. 6 in., to give the enginemen better vision from the cab front windows. Larger 5,500-gallon tenders have been fitted to some of the " Battle of Britain " engines to give an extended range of non-stop running.

With a tractive effort of 31,000 lb. at 85 per cent. boiler pressure, the "West Country" and " Battle of Britain " engines were more powerful than any Southern 4-6-0 or 4-4-0 passenger engines except the " Lord Nelsons," and they were rapidly adopted for main line work instead of the " King Arthurs " and " Schools." They could also run over lines on which " King Arthurs " and " Schools " were not permitted. Of the first 90 engines, 30 were allocated to Exmouth Junction, 15 each to Stewart's Lane and Ramsgate, 11 to Salisbury, 6 to Nine Elms, 5 to Plymouth Friary, 4 to Brighton, 3 to Dover and 1 to Eastleigh ; construction has been continued, mainly at Brighton works, to a total of 110 engines, but many changes of shed allocation have been made.

The engines based on Exmouth Junction and Plymouth, consisting mainly of the earlier numbers, handle the faster traffic west of Exeter, including the " Devon Belle " between Exeter and Ilfracombe. The Salisbury and Nine Elms engines have largely taken over trains formerly worked by " Arthurs " and " Nelsons " on the Western Division main lines, and, except for the " Belles," occasionally work " Merchant Navy " turns. The Salisbury engines also, in conjunction with the engines based on Brighton, work the through coast services. These trains use the Fareham-St. Denys section between Brighton and Southampton, over which no engine heavier than a Maunsell Mogul, or a " Schools " 4-4-0 subject to speed restriction, previously had been permitted to run. The Stewarts Lane, Ramsgate and Dover engines work boat trains and the Kent Coast traffic.

The first " West Country " 4-6-2 was placed in service in June, 1945, and was named at Exeter on July 10th, 1945. Engines of this type were introduced on the Ramsgate services on and from February 21st, 1946. In 1947, 21C119 *Bideford*, now No. 34019, was converted to oil burning, an oil fuelling plant having been installed at Exmouth Junction at the time when acute shortage of coal had brought oil-firing of locomotives into the limelight. *Bideford* was restored to coal burning in 1948. 21C136 (as yet unnamed), now No. 34036, also was converted to oil-fuel, using a different type of burner, and in this condition has hauled the "Atlantic Coast Express" between Waterloo and Exeter, taking water at Salisbury, in a very satisfactory manner; but the oil-burners later were removed from the firebox.

Besides being the first Pacifics to appear as far west as Padstow, and the first Pacific type to work regularly over the G.W.R. line between Exeter St. Davids and Plymouth *via* Newton Abbot (where the "Great Bear" was not allowed to run), the light Pacifics have appeared on many secondary routes such as the Somerset & Dorset line between Poole and Bath, the Oxted line, the Reading-Redhill line, and the Tattenham Corner branch, the latter with a Royal Special in 1947. As an experiment, No. 34059 *Sir Archibald Sinclair* worked over the Great Eastern Section of the Eastern Region for a short period during 1949, between Liverpool Street and both Norwich and Parkeston Quay, and put up some remarkable performances. But these were nothing to the exploits of Nos. 34004 *Yeovil*, 34005 *Barnstaple* and 34006 *Bude* in the Locomotive Exchanges of 1948, between Perth and Inverness, St. Pancras and Manchester Central, and Marylebone and Manchester respectively. When running on the Highland and Great Central lines, as described in Chapter 10, the Southern light Pacifics set up some entirely new standards of performance, and developed drawbar horsepowers over some sections that were the highest recorded throughout the exchange trials. Over the Great Eastern, Midland and Highland lines the Southern engines were the first Pacifics that have ever yet been permitted to run in ordinary passenger service. Finally, in the summer of 1951, three of these engines were drafted for a time to Stratford shed of the Great Eastern Section, for regular service between Liverpool Street and Norwich, in exchange for two new standard two-cylinder Pacifics of the "Britannia" class.

By proving their all-round usefulness, in addition to being capable of main line work not far short of "Merchant Navy" standards, the "Lightweights" may be regarded as even more successful than their bigger brothers, from the performance standpoint.

CHAPTER SIX

On A Pacific
Footplate

TO describe what the Southern Pacifics can do on the road is a congenial task. For as to their capabilities, when they are in good running condition and in competent hands, there can be no two opinions. Notwithstanding the limitation of driving wheel diameter to no more than 6 ft. 2 in., which in effect puts these engines into the " mixed traffic " category, it is safe to say that nothing faster on rails has yet appeared in Great Britain than the " Merchant Navy " and " West Country " 4-6-2s, and so far as concerns the Southern Region in particular, the performances of such outstanding previous express passenger classes as the 4-6-0 " Lord Nelsons " and " King Arthurs " and the 4-4-0 " Schools " have been outdistanced completely by the maximum achievements of the Pacifics.

This is not to say that in all respects the Bulleid Pacifics are ideal performers. Their addiction to slipping is a serious handicap, and the locomotive exchange trials of 1948 proved that both the larger and smaller Pacifics can display these slipping characteristics even when running at speed. On one run from Paddington to Plymouth, in climbing Rattery bank, west of Totnes, " Merchant Navy " Pacific No. 35019, as the dynamometer curve reveals, was slipping slightly but continuously up the final 1 in 90-95-65, and on entering Marley Tunnel the slipping became so severe that it was necessary to apply sand. As a result of sanding, the drawbar pull promptly rose from 6.53 to 7.44 tons. So far as concerns starting, however, with very careful handling the top link Southern drivers can get the engines away from a dead stand without slipping, even with heavy trains, as I have verified from the footplate even with so difficult an exit as that from Victoria Station up to the Grosvenor Bridge.

Throughout the exchange tests, also, the Southern drivers gave some most exemplary demonstrations of clean starting. Perhaps the most severe test was on the day when *Belgian Marine*, at the head of the down " Royal Scot," got stopped dead by signal just to the north of Tebay station, and the driver had to re-start his 505-ton train on Shap incline in very bad weather conditions. Fortunately the engine was on the 1 in 134 that precedes the 1 in 75, but even so there had to be some 2¼ minutes of cautious backing until Driver Swain could get his driving wheels in the right position to get away. The effect of the tendency to slip, therefore, is that the Southern Pacifics appear to the recorder to be sluggish starters, yet this is almost inevitable if slipping is to be avoided. But once the engines are well away, their performances often are brilliant to a degree, as is evident in the records that follow. The experience on Shap to which we have just referred was on one of the runs preliminary to the test week proper ; on one of the actual test runs *Belgian Marine* accelerated a 530-ton train on the 1 in 75 of Shap from 26½ to 29 m.p.h. without slipping, even though the drawbar pull to achieve this feat was mounting steadily from 6.18 to 8.60 tons.

As to the handling of the Southern Pacifics, to me the first journeys that I made on " Merchant Navy " and " West Country " Pacifics were a revelation. Their smoothness and quietness of running were superior to anything I had ever experienced previously. So much so, indeed, that where the engines were running under easy steam, the sound of the rail-joints, as we passed over them, was as readily audible as it would have been inside a coach in the train, and speed estimation by this means was possible with the greatest of ease, as also was the writing of my notes. It has been said that the quietness of the Bulleid 4-6-2s at speed is so marked on the footplate that engine-crews at times are deceived into thinking that they are travelling at a lower speed than is actually the case. Drivers have been known to offer this as an excuse when summoned on to " the carpet " to explain some over-spectacular piece of high speed running !

The care bestowed in the arrangement of the Bulleid cab, which has every control within the driver's reach without any necessity for him to rise from his seat, is most commendable ; the only defect in the cab layout was the position of the vacuum brake ejector, which cut off part of the driver's already rather restricted view of the road ahead, but in later engines the ejector has been moved, and the window enlarged.

Firing a Southern Pacific appears to be a matter of simplicity. " Opening out " one of these engines by way of a longer cut-off, or a wider regulator, with a corresponding sharpening of the blast, produces an immediate response from the boiler, as I saw with considerable surprise even when we were climbing so formidable an incline as Seaton bank, with the pressure *rising* rather than falling in the process ! To this lively steaming the thermic syphons in the firebox no doubt make a considerable contribution. Firing also seems to be facilitated considerably by the power-operated fire-door. It is a pleasure to watch the fire-door open like magic in front of the fireman's shovel, as he swings round from the tender and pivots lightly on his right heel, so depressing a pedal which admits steam to the small fire-door cylinder. Another special consideration for the crew is seen in the fluorescent dial markings of all the cab gauges, all made clearly visible after dark and in tunnels by ultra-violet light, so that there is no interference with the look-out ahead at night-time by lamps mounted in the cab. With such power at their command, crews of the Bulleid engines have little fear of heavy loads, even when it comes to a 575-ton " Devon Belle " to be hauled at express speeds over the tremendous gradients between Salisbury and Exeter.

For reasons already given, it is but rarely that the traveller on the footplate of a Southern 4-6-2 ever sees the regulator opened to anything like full. Like the " Lord Nelsons " and the " Schools," each Bulleid Pacific has a steam-chest pressure gauge (so rare a fitting on other British railways until then, and even since) as an essential requirement among the cab fittings of locomotives intended for express passenger service, and it is of great interest to note the continuous use to which the drivers put this informative piece of apparatus. It is, indeed, almost a temptation to " drive on the regulator " rather than by variation in both regulator openings and cut-off percentages to suit the various changes of gradient. In any event, the drivers appear to have their settled steam-chest pressures to suit each change of gradient, and to manipulate their regulator handles accordingly.

The higher boiler pressure of 280 lb. per sq. in. must be regarded as more in the nature of a reserve for contingencies than a continuous working figure, for a very large proportion of the work of the engines is done with no more than 110 to 150 lb. of steam in the steam-chests. However, this practice is in accord with what is becoming general in Great Britain, for the Official Report on the 1948 locomotive exchanges showed that full regulator working with very short cut-offs was unusual during the tests, even on the Western Region, where Churchward first built the engines which would respond to such handling and established the method as standard. On the rare occasions when the regulators of Southern 4-6-2s are opened fully, however, the steam-chest pressure creeps up to within 10 lb. or even 5 lb. of the boiler pressure, showing that the design of the steam passages is efficient, and that little energy is being lost in the passage of the steam from boiler to cylinders.

CHAPTER SEVEN

AT WORK ON THE BOURNEMOUTH LINE

M Y first acquaintance with a " Merchant Navy " footplate was when I joined Driver J. Swain and Fireman A. Fordrey, of Nine Elms (later to earn distinction by their work with Bulleid Pacifics over " foreign " lines in the 1948 exchanges) on No. 21C14 *Nederland Line* at the head of the down " Bournemouth Belle." We had not an outsize in loads ; the train comprised ten Pullmans, weighing 397 tons tare and 420 tons gross. Soon after starting, Swain notched up to 20 per cent., and between there and 15 per cent the cut-off stayed all the way to Southampton. A permanent way check brought us down to 20 m.p.h. after Wimbledon, and adverse signals caused a reduction to 45 before Surbiton, but after that the road was clear.

The run started with pressure up to 275 lb. in the boiler, but no more than 170 lb. was used in the steam-chest out to Clapham Junction, and then the regulator was closed still further. Yet, after the Surbiton check, with 20 per cent cut-off and 130 lb. in the steam-chest, our speed swept rapidly up until in the dip after Weybridge we were doing 75 m.p.h. Cut-off was then reduced to 15 per cent, and with 240 lb. of steam in the boiler and 130 lb. in the chest we went over milepost 31 summit at 66 m.p.h. After Fleet, Swain opened the engine out a little more, with 20 per cent cut-off and 150 lb. of steam in the steam-chest; this lifted our speed at 77½ m.p.h. beyond Hook, and the engine was then eased.

We had passed Woking, 24.4 miles from Waterloo, in 29 min. 19 sec., and the distance of 23.4 miles from Woking to Basingstoke was covered in 19 min. 58 sec. ; notwithstanding the extraordinarily easy conditions under which *Nederland Line* was being worked, indeed, we had reeled off the 35.8 miles from Surbiton through to Basingstoke at an average of 68.4 m.p.h. With the merest wisp of steam going down to the cylinders after we had begun the long downhill stretch past Winchester—speed was 74 m.p.h. at the maximum with no more than 60 lb. in the chest !—we ran into Southampton Central in 84 min. 10 sec. for the 79.2 miles, or 81 min. net. It was an easy matter to run on over the 28.7 miles from Southampton to Bournemouth Central in 34 min. 36 sec. start to stop.

As examples of the work of " Merchant Navy " Pacifics more fully extended, I give details in Table I of a couple of runs from Waterloo to Southampton, the first with the " Bournemouth Belle " made up to twelve cars, and the second a special test run made in the earlier days of this class, of which Mr. Bulleid was good enough to furnish me with the particulars. The comparison is interesting, because it shows that one of these engines would have little difficulty in repeating in ordinary day-to-day service the maximum achievement of a special test occasion.

Table I   WATERLOO—SOUTHAMPTON CENTRAL

Engine, "Merchant Navy" 4-6-2 No.			‡35019		§21C2	
Load, tons tare			490		517	
" " gross			515		520	
Distance			Times	Speeds	Times	Speeds
miles			min. sec.	m.p.h.	min. sec.	m.p.h.
0·0	WATERLOO		0 00	—	0 00	—
1·3	Vauxhall		3 59	40	3 45	38
3·9	CLAPHAM JUNCTION		7 41	46	7 30	*42
5·6	Earlsfield		9 41	56	9 44	56
7·3	Wimbledon		11 38	58	11 44	60
12·0	SURBITON		16 18	64/58	16 21	66
17·1	Walton		20 44	66	20 29	77
19·1	Weybridge		22 40	60	22 09	72
21·7	Byfleet		24 56	68½	24 11	77
					Sigs.	28
24·4	WOKING		27 26	62	27 00	—
28·0	Brookwood		31 22	55	31 29	48
31·0	Milepost 31		34 35	54	35 00	54
33·2	Farnborough		36 43	63	37 16	64
36·5	Fleet		39 35	70	40 18	68
39·7	Winchfield		42 27	66	43 00	69
42·2	Hook		44 33	67	45 00	75
			Sigs.	5		
47·8	BASINGSTOKE		54 10	—	49 31	64
50·3	Worting Junction		58 31	44	52 03	*46
58·1	Micheldever		66 48	74	60 00	76
66·6	WINCHESTER		72 58	86	66 45	74
69·7	Shawford		75 14	83/87	69 31	70
73·6	EASTLEIGH		77 53	84	72 30	70
75·9	Swaythling		79 38	78	74 43	68
77·3	St. Denys		Sigs.	10	75 44	65
78·1	Northam Junction		83 13	—	77 15	*13
79·2	SOUTHAMPTON CENTRAL		87 00	—	†79 31	*24
79·2	Net times (min.)		78	—	†77½	—

      * Speed restriction.   † Waterloo start to Southampton pass.
      ‡ French Line C.G.T.   § Union Castle (now No. 35002).

As bearing on what I have said in the previous chapter, the start of *French Line* on the first of the two runs was very gentle as far as Wimbledon, but the engine was then opened out, and the speed went up with a run from 49 to 64 m.p.h. in a short distance. The 30.2 miles from Surbiton to Hook, mainly " against the collar," were run in 28 min. 15 sec., but then came a very severe signal check. Again the recovery was taken very easily on the rising 1 in 249 grade, but once past the beginning of the long descent from Litchfield, the engine was given her head, and there was some very fast travelling, with a top speed of 87 m.p.h. near Winchester. But for a bad signal slowing at St. Denys, it should have been possible to complete the 79.2 miles to Southampton in 78 minutes without difficulty.

On the official test run the engine was obviously being worked harder, for the downhill speeds were very restrained, whereas the travel over the level and undulating stretches was much faster. The rise in speed from 64 m.p.h. at Wimbledon to 77 at Walton and Byfleet was notable, and not less so the 75 m.p.h. at Hook going west, with such a load as this. Just after Winchester " even time " from the start had been bettered, notwithstanding the signal check at Woking, and the passing time at Southampton Central was 79 min. 31 sec. This was a non-stop run to Bournemouth Central, and despite a second signal check, to 36 m.p.h. before Totton, it was completed in 112 min. 46 sec. from Waterloo, or 3¼ minutes less than the 116 minutes allowed the pre-war " Bournemouth Limited " to cover this 107.9 miles. The net time was not more than 109 minutes. Perhaps the most outstanding feature of this test was that *Union Castle* should have succeeded in working a

520-ton train to Bournemouth non-stop, at a net average of all but a mile-a-minute, on no more water than the 5,000 gallons carried in her six-wheel tender.

As companions to the down Southampton runs, I have set out in detail, in Table 2, a couple in the reverse direction, the first with the 7.30 a.m. from Bournemouth Central, timed by a correspondent who prefers to remain anonymous, and the second on the up " Bournemouth Belle," with a 12-car train, recorded by a friend whose name I have unfortunately mislaid. These runs show the capacity of the Southern Pacifics to continue running almost indefinitely over favourable stretches of track at sustained speeds of from 70 to well over 80 m.p.h.

In this direction there is a long grind from Allbrook Junction, Eastleigh, up to Litchfield box—16½ miles right off at 1 in 252—and *Elders Fyffes*, in the first run, had to start a 480-ton train in the middle of it. This was done successfully with speed rising to 50½ m.p.h. ; on another similarly loaded run No. 35020 started more cautiously out of Winchester, but tied in time up to Litchfield with an attained speed of 56 m.p.h. On the second run tabulated, with the Pullman, *Nederland Line* had no Winchester stop ; the long climb was begun at 55 m.p.h., and speed crept gradually up to 58 m.p.h. with this 515-ton load, a performance which would require an equivalent drawbar horsepower output of at least 1,900. After making slight speed reductions over the junction at Worting, both drivers let themselves go over the galloping ground from Basingstoke ; the times on to Hampton

Table 2   SOUTHAMPTON CENTRAL—WATERLOO

		†35016		‡35014	
Engine " Merchant Navy " 4-6-2 No.		†35016		‡35014	
Load, tons tare		438		490	
,, ,, gross		480		515	
Distance		Times	Speeds	Distance	Times	Speeds
miles		min. sec.	m.p.h.	miles	min. sec.	m.p.h.
0·0	SOUTHAMPTON CENTRAL	0 00	—	0·0	0 00	—
1·1	Northam Junction	3 13	*22/47	1·1	3 27	—
1·9	St. Denys	p.w.s.	25	1·9	5 02	43
5·6	EASTLEIGH	10 47	—	5·6	9 42	53½
9·5	Shawford	15 36	49	9·5	13 47	56
12·6	WINCHESTER	{ 19 44	—	—	pass	—
0·0		{ 0 00	—	12·6	17 10	56
2·1	Winchester Junction	4 51	41	14·7	19 24	56½
4·8	Wallers Ash	8 23	47	17·4	22 15	57¼
8·5	Micheldever	12 46	50	21·1	26 00	58
10·3	Litchfield	15 03	50½/60	22·9	27 58	57/68
16·3	Worting Junction	21 25	*50	28·9	33 33	*60
18·8	BASINGSTOKE	23 57	65½	31·4	35 55	67
24·4	Hook	28 35	75/72	37·0	40 20	79/76½
26·9	Winchfield	30 29	76	39·5	42 12	80¼
30·1	Fleet	33 02	79	42·7	44 42	79
33·4	Farnborough	35 33	76	46·0	47 17	75
35·6	Milepost 31	37 19	74½	48·2	49 07	75
38·6	Brookwood	39 35	83½	51·2	51 30	82
42·2	WOKING	42 21	*70	54·8	54 24	*69
44·9	Byfleet	44 34	76	57·5	56 41	75
47·5	Weybridge	46 39	69	60·1	58 47	72½
49·5	Walton	48 22	73½	62·1	60 30	74
		eased				
53·3	Hampton Court Junction	51 32	66	65·9	63 32	74
54·6	SURBITON	52 46	61	67·2	64 33	—
59·3	Wimbledon	57 07	70½	71·9	69 11	68
62·7	CLAPHAM JUNCTION	60 22	*40	75·3	72 18	*40
		Sigs.	—			
66·6	WATERLOO	68 02	—	79·2	79 08	—
66·6	Net times (min.)	66½	—	79·2	79	—

* Speed restriction.   † *Elders Fyffes*.   ‡ *Nederland Line*.

Court Junction tied almost to the second, and required both engines to keep up an average speed of 75 m.p.h. for 34½ miles right off with these weighty trains. So *Nederland Line* ran the 79.2 miles from Southampton to Waterloo in 79 min. 8 sec., and *Elders Fyffes* the 66.6 miles from Winchester in a net time of no more than 66½ minutes. I may add that on another up run with the " Bournemouth Belle," loaded to 500 tons, as recorded by Mr. A. C. Horner and Mr. J. Press, No. 35012 *United States Line* accelerated to and maintained a steady 59 to 61 m.p.h. all the way up the 1 in 252 from Winchester to Litchfield.

CHAPTER EIGHT

FROM SALISBURY TO EXETER

BOTH on test runs and in ordinary service, however, it is over the heavy grades between Salisbury and Exeter that the " Merchant Navy " Pacifics have performed some of their most spectacular feats. This well-aligned 88-miles length, free from all speed restrictions other than that through Wilton, just west of Salisbury, permits very high maximum speeds without hindrance, and with gradients as steep as 1 in 80, and loads which in summer may exceed the 500-ton mark, a good deal of dependence is placed on the impetus from the down gradients to carry the expresses up the subsequent rising grades. On the other hand, if the engines have to start from Templecombe, Yeovil Junction or Seaton Junction, in the westbound direction, or from Axminster or Sherborne coming east, they have to face very difficult uphill conditions, from Seaton Junction and Sherborne in particular.

In the spring of 1942, less than a year after her construction, No. 21C3 *Royal Mail* (now No. 35003) showed what could be done with a load of 517 tons on a test run from Exeter to Yeovil Junction and back, timed by Mr. A. Earle Edwards. The run of 48.9 miles was completed in 49 min. 56 sec. eastbound and 49 min. 5 sec. westbound. On the latter, the engine ran the 14.1 miles from Hewish Crossing to Seaton Junction, mainly downhill, at an average of 77.6 m.p.h., and then climbed the formidable Seaton bank—1½ miles at 1 in 100, 4¼ miles at 1 in 80, and ½-mile at 1 in 132 through Honiton tunnel—without the speed dropping below 40 m.p.h. As a result, the 14.9 miles from Axminster to Sidmouth Junction, right over Honiton summit, were covered in 14 min. 10 sec., at an average of over a mile-a-minute with this weighty train. This was an early foretaste of what later would become a by no means unusual performance with the even heavier " Devon Belle " at week-ends.

In the years 1946 and 1947, two further eastbound test runs were made, and I am able to give details of these also by the courtesy of Mr. Bulleid. These journeys were probably the fastest that have ever been made between Exeter and Salisbury ; they figure in Table 3. The first run, made by *Nederland Line*, was with a 12-coach train, and the net time of 81½ minutes for the 88 miles was 18½ minutes less than the fastest pre-war non-stop schedule eastbound. The uphill running was remarkable, as is clear in such averages as 69.2 m.p.h. all the way from Axminster up to Hewish Crossing, 58.4 m.p.h. from Whimple to the west end of Honiton tunnel—a stretch that finishes with 4¾ miles at 1 in 100-90—and 63.4 and 63.1 m.p.h. up the sharp climbs from Sherborne to Milborne Port and Gillingham to Semley respectively.

As for the speeds made by *Blue Funnel* with the lighter 10-coach train of 345 tons, they were simply electrifying. Reaching 74 m.p.h. down the short descent from Exmouth Junction past Pinhoe, the engine carried the 5 miles up to milepost 161¼ (1 in 170-135-145-100) at a minimum of 58 m.p.h., and the steeper 4¾ miles to Honiton tunnel, 1 in 100-90 as just mentioned, at the almost incredible minimum of 62 m.p.h., so reaching the tunnel in a few seconds over 20 minutes from the Exeter start. Before Seaton Junction speed rose to 96 m.p.h. ; after an easing to 78 m.p.h. round the curve here, a further maximum of 86 preceded the astonishing average of 73.4 m.p.h. all the way up from Axminster to Hewish Crossing, the minimum even on the final 1 in 200-100-160 being 67 m.p.h. Then came another 90 m.p.h. maximum, through Crewkerne, before the Yeovil Junction stop, the time to which, 48.9 miles from Exeter, was 44 min. 14 sec. The best existing schedule for the same run is one hour. Delays spoiled the remainder of this run ; but were the time of *Blue Funnel* from Exeter to Sutton Bingham added to that of *Nederland Line* from there to Salisbury, the total obtained is no more than 78 min. 22 sec. over these 88 miles of exceptionally heavy gradients.

In their heyday, the " King Arthur " 4-6-0s were limited nominally to 360 tare tons on the fastest timings, but often handled considerably heavier loads than this ;

Table 3

S.R. TEST RUNS,—EXETER—SALISBURY

Distance	Engine No.	†21C14 389 415	‡21C13 325 345
	Load, tons tare		
	,, ,, gross		
miles		min. sec.	min. sec.
0·0	EXETER CENTRAL	0 00	0 00
1·1	*Exmouth Junction*	3 32	3 25
2·9	Pinhoe	6 02	5 51
4·8	Broad Clyst	7 47	7 30
8·5	Whimple	11 12	10 50
12·2	SIDMOUTH JUNCTION ...	15 20	14 40
16·8	Honiton	19 38	18 37
18·2	*Honiton Tunnel West End* ...	21 10	20 04
23·8	Seaton Junction	26 04	24 11
27·0	Axminster	28 44	26 35
32·1	Chard Junction	32 58	30 33
37·5	*Hewish Crossing*	37 50	35 10
		Sigs.	
40·1	Crewkerne	42 15	37 15
		Sigs.	
46·7	Sutton Bingham	49 33	41 55
48·9	YEOVIL JUNCTION ...	Pass	44 14
		51 20	0 00
53·5	Sherborne	55 05	6 32
57·2	Milborne Port	58 35	10 28
59·6	TEMPLECOMBE	60 45	12 46
			p.w.s.
66·4	Gillingham	66 31	21 13
70·5	Semley	70 25	26 23
75·5	Tisbury	74 55	31 16
79·8	Dinton	78 14	34 52
85·5	Wilton*	82 40	39 53
			p.w.s.
88·0	SALISBURY	86 06	44 51
88·0	Net times (min.)	81½	44½+39¾

* Speed restriction.   † Nederland Line.   ‡ Blue Funnel.

the most outstanding record is probably that of Driver Young of Salisbury, who in 1934, with No. 768 *Sir Balin*, worked a 13-coach load of 421 tare tons (460 tons tare) from Salisbury to Exeter in precisely 90 minutes, running the 69.4 miles from Semley to Exmouth Junction in 63 min. 55 sec., and completing the 1 in 80 up to Honiton tunnel at 26½ m.p.h. without the slightest shortage of steam. But a " King Arthur " could not have looked at the week-end load of the " Devon Belle," more than 100 tons heavier, when 14 Pullmans are run, weighing 545 tons tare and at least 575 tons with a full complement of passengers and luggage. What a " Merchant Navy " Pacific can do with such a train is set out in Table 4 ; the run concerned was timed by Dr. J. L. Fluker. It begins, of course, not at Salisbury, but at Wilton, where engines of this train are changed.

Up the rising grades to Semley the start was fairly gentle, but *Cunard-White Star* was then extended sufficiently to permit an average speed of 70.4 m.p.h. over the next 38.4 miles

THE
LIGHT PACIFICS—

Right :
" West Country "
No. 21C101 Exeter as
built.

[British Railways

Left : No. 21C105 *Barnstaple* at Brighton in 1946, fitted with indicator shelter for testing after modification of smoke deflectors to the new standard length.

Below : No. 34019 *Bideford* was one of the light Pacifics fitted for oil burning.

[H. M. Madgwick, F. F. Moss

Below : The " Battle of Britain " engines appeared with a modified cab. No. 34076 *41 Squadron* approaches Faversham with a Ramsgate-Victoria express, April 23rd, 1949. (Note " D1 " 4-4-0 No. 31545 also in motion on the same line, preparatory to diverging at the turnout ahead of it, with a Dover-Faversham local train.)

[Rev. A. W. V. Mace

FROM EAST TO WEST—Light Pacifics a
sometimes seen on the Oxted line ; "We
Country" No. 34036 (unnamed) pass
Upper Warlingham (*left*) with the 4.50 p.r
Victoria-Brighton (via Oxted) train c
June 10th, 1950. They are now no strange
on the "Bournemouth Belle" ; "Battle
Britain" No. 34061 *73 Squadron* pass
Lymington Junction with the down expre
on May 29th, 1950 (*below*).

[*R. K. Kirkland, J. C. Flemo*

On special occasio
the light Pacifics pen
trate the electric area
"West Country" N
21C129 (unname
heads through Purl
for Tattenham Corn
on June 7th, 194
with a special co
veying T.M. the Ki
and Queen to t
Oaks at Epsom (*lef*

[*B. J. Hold*

FROM EAST TO WEST—Through interchange workings with the W.R., light Pacifics work regularly over the old G.W. main line from Exeter to Plymouth. "West Country" No. 34019 *Bideford* (*above*) near the summit of Dainton bank with a down stopping train composed of L.M.R. stock. One of the heaviest duties on the Eastern Section (now performed by "Merchant Navies") is the "Night Ferry." "Battle of Britain" No. 21C157 *Biggin Hill* heads the up train past Folkestone.   [*J. G. Hubback, Rev. A. C. Cawston*

A STUDY OF POWER—" West Country " Pacific No. 21C139 tackles the bank out of Victoria with a Kent Coast express.
[*Eric Treacy*

46

LOCOMOTIVE
ANGES, 1948—To pro-
ater pick-up apparatus
ating S.R. Pacifics were
with L.M.R. tenders
020, the standby engine,
notographed at South-
(*right*) ; note the
neter fitting to the rear
wheel. No. 34004
was the "West Country"
the Scottish Region and
(*centre*) waiting to leave
with the 4 p.m. express
rness on July 15th, 1948 ;
ablet-catching apparatus
o the cab ; and (*bottom*)
ng south over Shap as
o L.M.R. "Royal Scot"
63 *Civil Service Rifleman*
Perth-Euston express
y 12th, 1948.

Moss, C. Herbert, E. Treacy

MISCELLANY

May, 1949,
34059 *Sir Arch*
Sinclair was teste
the ex-G.E. main
and is seen (*abov*
Norwich with th
" Norfolkman "
May 18th, 1
No. 35005 *Can*
Pacific, fitted
mechanical sto
was at Rugby
February, 1950
for trials on the
Test Plant there.

In May, 1950, light Pacifics
appeared north of the
Thames with specials for
a football match at
Wembley. One of them
was No. 34084 (un-
named), which was photo-
graphed (*right*) with a
special from Dover on
the North & South West
Junction line at Neasden.

[*E. G. Dott*

to Chard Junction, including minimum speeds as high as 58 m.p.h. up Templecombe bank, 58½ up Sutton Bingham bank, and 52 up the 1 in 80 of Crewkerne bank. These climbs were assisted by the impetus from such high speeds as 83 m.p.h. before Templecombe, 87 at Sherborne, and an unusually speedy 80 just before Crewkerne. Nemesis next overtook the " Belle " in the shape of a dead stand for signals at Broom Crossing, beyond Chard Junction, with the 54.9 miles to this point completed in 53 min. 23 sec. start to stop. The offending train was doubtless stowed in the loop at Seaton Junction, for there was a further check to 15 m.p.h. through Axminster, but after that the road was clear.

The Pacific now accelerated very rapidly to 58 m.p.h. at the bottom of the dip beyond Axminster, and then climbed to Seaton bank so admirably that Honiton tunnel was entered at 27 m.p.h. Moreover, there was obviously no suggestion of slipping, as speed increased to 33 m.p.h. in the tunnel. In the end, though fully 8 minutes had been lost by the checks, Sidmouth Junction was reached a minute early. The 73.3 miles had been run in 74 minutes net ; and had the run been from Salisbury (instead of Wilton) to Exeter, I have little doubt that the Pacific could have completed it in 89 minutes with 575 tons, as compared with the maximum " King Arthur " effort of 90 minutes with 460 tons. That

Table 4

" DEVON BELLE," WILTON—EXETER

Engine : No. 21C4 *Cunard-White Star.*
Load : 14 Pullmans, 546 tons tare, 575 tons gross.

Distance			Times	Speeds
miles			min. sec.	m.p.h.
0·0	WILTON	... ...	0 00	—
5·7	Dinton	... ...	9 19	60/55
10·0	Tisbury	... ...	13 53	57
15·0	Semley	... ...	19 15	48½
19·1	Gillingham	... ...	22 47	79
21·4	*Milepost 107½* ...	... ...	24 39	64
23·7	*Milepost 109¾* ...	... ...	26 27	83
25·9	TEMPLECOMBE	... ...	28 11	—
27·4	*Milepost 113½* ...	... ...	29 40	58
32·0	Sherborne	... ...	33 22	87
36·6	YEOVIL JUNCTION	... ...	36 48	76
39·9	*Milepost 126* ...	... ...	39 57	58½
43·9	*Milepost 130* ...	... ...	43 16	80
45·4	Crewkerne	... ...	44 23	—
46·9	*Milepost 133* ...	... ...	46 02	52
53·4	Chard Junction	... ...	51 44	77
			Sig. stop	
58·5	Axminster	... ...	61 29	15/58
61·7	Seaton Junction	... ...	62 58	50
66·4	*Milepost 152½* ...	... ...	73 44	27
67·4	*Milepost 153½* ...	... ...	75 45	33
68·7	Honiton	... ...	77 11	58
71·9	*Milepost 158* ...	... ...	—	70
73·3	SIDMOUTH JUNCTION	... ...	82 07	—
1·7	*Milepost 161¼* ...	... ...	3 42	45
3·7	*Whimple*	... ...	5 42	68
7·4	Broad Clyst ...	... ...	8 39	79
11·1	*Exmouth Junction*	... ...	12 06	—
12·2	EXETER	... ...	14 55	—

this is no isolated feat is proved by a " Devon Belle " run in the reverse direction, timed by Rev. P. A. Lushington, when No. 35003 *Royal Mail* worked a load of 13 Pullmans (508 tons tare and 535 tons gross) from Sidmouth Junction to Wilton in an actual time of 74 min. 32 sec., attaining " even time " by Dinton (67.6 miles in 67 min. 48 sec. from the start).

As to the methods used by drivers in working Pacifics over this route, there are considerable variations. On a footplate journey that I made on No. 21C5 with the down " Atlantic Coast Express " in the autumn of 1946, Driver Millman of Exmouth Junction liked fairly long cut-offs and restricted regulator openings. On most of the rising grades 40 per cent cut-off was the order of the day, increased to 45 per cent up the final 1 in 80 to Honiton tunnel ; but the regulator opening allowed no more than 160 to 180 lb. pressure in the steam-chests on these grades, except up Seaton bank, where the regulator at last was opened to full, or very nearly, and steam-chest pressure increased to 255 lb. The fireman filled the firebox to such an extent that by Templecombe the boiler pressure had fallen from the 270 lb. with which we started to 190 lb. ; but every harder effort by the locomotive, by sharpening the blast, caused the pressure to rise, and it was astonishing indeed, as already mentioned in Chapter 6, to see the needle of the gauge climbing steadily from 250 to 275 lb. up the first half of the strenuous Seaton bank climb, with a drop again to 250 lb. before we had breasted the summit. The weight of the train was 475 tons, and Sidmouth Junction was reached in 84 min. 26 sec. from Salisbury, $5\frac{1}{2}$ minutes early ; minimum speed at Honiton tunnel was 28 m.p.h., and the highest speeds reached at any point were from 75 to $77\frac{1}{2}$ m.p.h.

On a run described by Dr. J. L. Fluker in the *Railway Magazine* of November, 1948, however, Driver Lethbridge of Exmouth Junction, with No. 21C3 *Royal Mail* and 15 coaches of 525 gross tons as compared with our 475 tons, was an exponent of working at much shorter cut-offs and wider regulator openings. Up the long initial ascent from Salisbury to Semley, for example, the engine was working at 30 per cent as far as Dinton and 25 per cent from there to Semley, with boiler pressure at 250 to 265 lb. and steam-chest pressure rising from 200 to 255 lb. ; up the other principal banks 25 per cent cut-off and from 200 to 260 lb. steam-chest pressures were the general method, until Seaton bank was reached, where cut-off was advanced gradually from 23 per cent at

Table 5

3 P.M. EX-WATERLOO, SALISBURY—EXETER

Engine : Class " MN," No. 35014, *Nederland Line.*
Load to Templecombe : 8 coaches, 269 tons tare, 290 tons gross.
Load from Templecombe : 6 coaches, 202 tons tare, 215 tons gross.

Distance		Schedule	Times	Speeds
miles		min.	min. sec.	m.p.h.
0·0	SALISBURY	0	0 00	—
2·5	Wilton	—	5 24	—
8·2	Dinton	—	11 10	70½/65
12·5	Tisbury	—	15 06	69
17·5	Semley	—	19 49	58½
21·6	Gillingham	—	23 08	79
23·9	Milepost 107½	—	25 03	64½
27·2	Milepost 110½	—	27 44	82
28·4	TEMPLECOMBE	34	29 18	—
1·5	Milepost 113½	—	4 00	33
2·4	Milborne Port	—	5 08	—
6·1	Sherborne	—	8 18	80½
			p.w.s.	*30
10·7	YEOVIL JUNCTION	—	13 57	66
12·9	Sutton Bingham	—	16 02	60
14·3	Milepost 126½	—	17 25	60
16·0	Hardington	—	18 50	82
19·5	Crewkerne	—	21 33	—
21·3	Milepost 126½	—	23 25	55
27·5	Chard Junction	—	28 21	80½/77½
32·6	AXMINSTER	—	32 19	82
35·8	Seaton Junction	—	34 50	72½
40·6	Milepost 152½	—	39 52	51
41·6	Milepost 153½	—	41 02	52
42·8	Honiton	—	42 07	75
46·4	Milepost 158½	—	44 57	80½
47·4	SIDMOUTH JUNCTION ...	53	46 16	—
3·7	Whimple	—	4 49	74
7·4	Broad Clyst	—	7 35	85
9·3	Pinhoe	—	9 04	70½
11·1	Exmouth Junction	12	10 40	†62½
12·2	EXETER	15	13 00	—

* Speed restriction.   † On shutting off steam.

Seaton Junction to 40 per cent from milepost 151 to the summit at milepost 153½. The boiler pressure up this arduous stretch kept steadily at 260-270 lb., and steam-chest pressure at 250-260 lb., showing that the regulator was full open, except after entering Honiton tunnel, when the regulator was brought back to correct some slipping on the greasy rails. On the easy and downhill lengths, 18 to 20 per cent cut-off was the general practice, with the merest wisp of steam passing through the main steam-pipe.

These methods of working were considerably more than sufficient for timekeeping ; speeds were 57 m.p.h. over Semley summit (a fine piece of work), 82 at Gillingham, 44 at the top of Templecombe bank, and 75 at Sherborne, after which came a bad permanent way slowing, to 15 m.p.h., at Sutton Bingham. At Hewish summit the minimum was

38 m.p.h., and 79 through Axminster was followed by 28 on entering Honiton tunnel and 26 on leaving it. The 75.8 miles from Salisbury to Sidmouth Junction were run in 87 min. 30 sec., or 84 minutes net, roughly equal to the unchecked 84½ minutes of my own journey described in the previous paragraph.

A brilliant example of time recovery with a lighter train is seen in Table 5. The 3 p.m. from Waterloo to Exeter had been delayed, and when Driver Puncher, of Exmouth Junction shed, took over No. 35014 at Salisbury, it was with a late start, by the working time, of 17 minutes. Yet notwithstanding a permanent way check beyond Sherborne, all the lost time was regained except a trifling ¾-min. It is true that the load was almost negligible for an engine of such power, especially west of Templecombe, where no more than 6 coaches remained, of 215 tons gross ; but even so, to climb the 1 in 80 to Hewish Summit at a minimum of 55 m.p.h., and the 4½ miles at the same inclination to Honiton tunnel at a minimum of 51 m.p.h., was an astonishing experience. With 8 coaches of 290 tons weight, also, the 58½ m.p.h. minimum up the 1 in 145 to Semley summit was a fine achievement.

Downhill the accelerations were extremely rapid, but speed was not allowed much to exceed 80 m.p.h. at any point ; nevertheless there were six well-separated " eighties " at different stages of the run. Perhaps the most outstanding time was 8 min. 43 sec. for the 9.0 miles from Axminster to Honiton summit (milepost 153½) ; another notable time was 31 minutes exactly for the 35.7 miles from Yeovil Junction to milepost 158¼, Hewish and Honiton summits both included. The quickest start of the journey was from Sidmouth Junction, the 11.1 miles to Exmouth Junction being covered in 10 min. 40 sec. The total net gain in running was 16 minutes, and on such form as this there is little doubt that the engine could have run the 88 miles from Salisbury to Exeter, with a clear road, in 81 minutes.

One further experimental run with a " Merchant Navy " Pacific remains to be chronicled : it was made in 1945 by No. 21C2 *Union Castle* with a load of 454 tons tare, 460 tons gross, from Victoria to Dover Marine. The exit from London by this route is extremely difficult ; the engine was slowed to 30 m.p.h. at Herne Hill, 44 at Kent House, and 23 at Bickley Junction, but even so managed to reach 60 m.p.h. on the brief descent to Shortlands, and thus got through Orpington, 14.9 miles, in 20 min. 38 sec., and Knockholt, 17.7 miles, in 24 min. 26 sec., clearing the summit at 48. But there was a 20 m.p.h. signal check before Dunton Green, and after a brief 78 m.p.h. past Hildenborough, an extremely drastic 32 m.p.h. slack through Tonbridge was followed by a 20 m.p.h. permanent way slowing.

Not until Paddock Wood was it possible to give the engine her head, and then came a grand sprint at 77 to 85 m.p.h., on practically level track ; the 29.4 miles from Paddock Wood to Westenhanger were run at an average of 78.6 m.p.h., and the 3.3 miles from Staplehurst to Headcorn at 86.7 m.p.h. average. Sandling Junction, 66.5 miles from Victoria, was passed in 68 min. 44 sec., despite the checks, but further slowings and a signal stop made the time for the 78.0 miles to Dover Marine 84 min. 55 sec. Net time, however, was 77½ minutes, whereas the test schedule had allowed 90 minutes for the run. From the particulars that have been given, it is clear that the " Merchant Navy " Pacifics are more than masters of their work, and that even when the maximum demands are made on them, they still have plenty in hand.

CHAPTER NINE

THE LIGHT PACIFICS
AT WORK

AT first the " West Country " and " Battle of Britain " Pacifics, having been built for secondary duties, got less opportunity than their more powerful relations for displaying their prowess, but as by degrees they have been drafted to some of the more important sheds, they have been found fully capable of undertaking many of the " Merchant Navy " duties, and have proved themselves extremely capable engines in relation to their size and weight.

In the autumn of 1946 I had my first journey on the footplate of an engine of this type, when I rode with Driver F. Rickwood and Fireman J. Chessun, of Stewart's Lane shed, on No. 21C135 from Victoria to Dover Marine with the down *Golden Arrow*. It was a pleasant October day, and the load of 368 tons tare and 390 tons gross proved no more than a plaything for the locomotive.

At our exit, in the extremely difficult conditions of the 1 in 62 climb from Victoria on to the Grosvenor Bridge, it was pleasant to note that a Southern Pacific *can* be started without an atom of slip ; this certainly was the case with Driver Rickwood's handling of his regulator. The usual handicaps of this slack-infested and heavily-graded exit from London were added to by a signal check before Brixton and a permanent way slowing to walking pace after Herne Hill, but despite these slowings and a cautious 35 m.p.h. over the junctions at Bickley and Petts Wood and the connecting loop, we were through Orpington 2 minutes early, in 25 min. 54 sec. for the 14.9 miles from Victoria. Up the long 1 in 100 climbs to Sydenham Hill and past Bromley South and Bickley, the engine was worked at cut-offs of 45 and 40 per cent respectively, with the regulator well open, so that of 260 to 270 lb. in the boiler there was from 200 to 230 lb. in the steam-chests. We touched 66 m.p.h. at Dunton Green, were slowed to 45 through Sevenoaks, attained $70\frac{1}{2}$ at Hildenborough, and then were brought down to 35 for Tonbridge curve, after which came a permanent way slowing to 15 before Paddock Wood.

Now at last, on the fine straight stretch towards Ashford, the engine could be permitted some speeding. With cut-off fixed at 25 per cent, and regulator full open, our speed mounted rapidly to 66 m.p.h. at Marden and $77\frac{1}{2}$ at Headcorn ; then Rickwood brought his regulator back to give 185 to 190 lb. pressure in the steam-chests out of the 230-240 lb. in the boiler, but speed still held at precisely the same level, of 75 to a maximum of 79 m.p.h. all the way to Ashford ; in fact, we averaged 73.3 m.p.h. throughout over the 21 undulating miles from Marden to Smeeth, and $\frac{3}{4}$-minute ahead of time at Paddock Wood thus increased to $2\frac{3}{4}$ minutes ahead by Ashford. The rest of the run was made, therefore, with the regulator brought still further back, but even 115 to 120 lb. in the steam-chests was enough to maintain a minimum of 60 m.p.h. up the long rise to Westenhanger. Sandling Junction, 65.4 miles, was passed in 80 min. 2 sec., 4 minutes early ; then followed a slowing through Folkestone and a permanent way check in the Warren ; but we came to rest at Dover Marine, 76.9 miles, in 96 min. 38 sec. from Victoria, just under 3½ minutes ahead of time. The net time on this effortless run, which is set out in detail in Table 6, may be put at 88 or 89 minutes.

The ability of a "West Country" 4-6-2 to steam continuously at high speed is well illustrated in the run which figures in Table 7, timed by the late Mr. R. E. Charlewood. Curiously enough, the engine was the same as the one on which I rode with the "Golden Arrow" to Dover, though now with the number changed from 21C135 to 34035, bearing the name *Shaftesbury*, and transferred to the Western Division. The train was the tightly-timed 7.30 a.m. from Exeter to Waterloo, one of the very few long-distance trains of the late Southern Railway that have been restored to their full pre-war scheduled speeds.

Nothing outstanding was done between Salisbury and Andover ; it was from the re-start at Andover Junction that interest began. At the top of the 3¼ miles at 1 in 176 to the 62½ milepost the engine had accelerated her 385-ton

Table 6

"GOLDEN ARROW," VICTORIA—DOVER

Engine : "West Country" 4-6-2 No. 21C135.
Load : 368 tons tare, 390 tons gross.

Distance		Schedule	Actual	Speed
miles		min.	min. sec.	m.p.h.
0·0	VICTORIA	0	0 00	—
1·9	Wandsworth Road	—	5 02	—
			Sigs.	
3·2	Brixton	7	7 24	—
4·0	HERNE HILL	8½	9 07	*28
			p.w.s.	*5
5·7	Sydenham Hill	—	12 50	—
7·2	Penge	—	15 58	49
8·7	Beckenham Junction	17	17 50	38
10·9	BROMLEY SOUTH	—	20 07	51
12·6	*Bickley Junction*	23	22 45	*35
13·4	*Petts Wood Junction*	25	24 04	*33
14·9	ORPINGTON	28	25 54	—
16·4	Chelsfield	—	27 56	46
17·7	Knockholt	—	29 39	39½
21·7	Dunton Green	—	34 07	66
23·2	SEVENOAKS	39	35 42	*45
23·8	*North End Sevenoaks Tunnel* ...	—	36 27	45
28·1	Hildenborough	—	41 11	70½
30·6	TONBRIDGE	47	44 15	*35
			p.w.s.	*15
35·9	Paddock Wood	53½	52 45	—
40·5	Marden	—	57 42	66
43·0	Staplehurst	—	59 54	—
46·3	Headcorn	—	62 32	77½/75
51·5	Pluckley	—	66 46	79/75
55·0	*Chart Siding*	—	69 36	72½
57·2	ASHFORD	74	71 13	77½
61·5	Smeeth	—	74 55	67
65·3	Westenhanger	—	78 32	60
66·5	Sandling Junction	84	80 02	*50
69·2	*Cheriton Junction*	—	83 18	60
71·0	FOLKESTONE CENTRAL ...	—	85 13	*50
72·0	Folkestone Junction	90	86 22	—
			p.w.s.	*20
78·0	DOVER MARINE	100	96 38	—

* Speed restriction.

load to 45 m.p.h. ; a mile-a-minute average was sustained up the gradual rise past Overton ; then, from Worting Junction, there began a tremendous burst of speed, with from 76 to 81½ m.p.h. sustained as far as Woking (save for the slight drop to 73 over the " hump " at milepost 31), and an average speed of 76.5 m.p.h. throughout over the 38.3 miles from Worting to Surbiton. A series of signal checks hampered the running from Surbiton to Wimbledon, but even so Waterloo, 66.4 miles from Andover, was reached in 66 min. 23 sec. The net time for the journey was certainly not more than 63½ minutes.

With a heavier train of 13 bogies, 430 tons tare and 450 tons gross, another correspondent (whose name unfortunately I have mislaid) timed a similar feat by No. 34109 *Sir Trafford Leigh Mallory* on an up Bournemouth express. The engine had taken matters fairly easily up the long 1 in 250 to Litchfield summit ; from Shawford to Micheldever the speed had ranged between 50 and 45 m.p.h., and then followed a permanent way slowing to 22 m.p.h., so that it took 19 min. 2 sec. to pass Winchester, 12.6 miles from Southampton Central, and 40 min. 37 sec. to Worting Junction, 28.9 miles. Now came the speed once again—73 m.p.h. before and 70 after Hook, 75 before Farnborough and 65 over milepost 31, 74 at Brookwood and 70-71 on to Byfleet, where the engine was eased, after 28.7 miles had been run at an average of all but 73 m.p.h. with this 450-ton train. Basingstoke, 31.4 miles, was passed in 43 min. 4 sec. ; the 23.4 miles on to Woking occupied 19 min. 11 sec. and the 12.4 miles thence to Surbiton 11 min. 10 sec. ; and the passing of Clapham Junction, 75.3 miles, in 82 min. 35 sec. should have got the train into Waterloo in about 89½ minutes but for signal checks. The net time was 87¼ minutes for the 79.2 miles.

As showing the extra-ordinary accelerative powers of one of the light Pacifics, I cannot do better than quote some details of a run with the 10.35 a.m. out of Waterloo timed, on a summer Saturday in 1950, by Mr. H. T. W. Clements. The engine was No. 34063 and the load a relatively modest 295 tons tare, or 310 tons with passengers and luggage. Very soon after starting, between Vauxhall and Clapham Junction, there was a signal check to 3 m.p.h., but in two miles the engine was up

Table 7

ANDOVER JUNCTION—WATERLOO

Distance	Engine : " West Country " 4-6-2 No. 34035, *Shaftesbury.* Load : 366 tons tare, 385 tons gross.		
miles		min. sec.	m.p.h.
0·0	ANDOVER JUNCTION	0 00	—
3·8	Milepost 62¼	7 11	45
7·2	Whitchurch	10 48	—
10·8	Overton	14 24	—
16·1	Worting Junction	19 34	67
18·6	BASINGSTOKE	21 39	—
24·2	Hook	25 58	80/76
33·2	Farnborough	32 52	80
35·4	Milepost 31	34 39	73
38·4	Brookwood	37 02	81¼
42·0	WOKING	39 45	81
47·3	Weybridge	43 41	eased
53·1	Hampton Court Junction	48 26	—
54·4	SURBITON	49 36	—
		Sigs.	
59·1	Wimbledon	55 56	—
62·5	CLAPHAM JUNCTION	60 35	—
66·4	WATERLOO	66 23	—

to 50 m.p.h., by Wimbledon to 62 and by Hampton Court Junction, 13.3 miles out, to 75 ; then, after a slight relapse to 72 at Weybridge, to no less than 81 at Byfleet Junction.

Nemesis followed in the shape of a signal check to walking pace at Byfleet, but having got the road, the driver again whipped his mount to 55 m.p.h. up 2.7 miles at 1 in 387 to Woking, and further to 69 up the 1 in 326-314 past Brookwood, only to meet a third signal check, to 30 m.p.h., near milepost 31. From here there was yet another terrific acceleration to 70 m.p.h. at Fleet and 80 at Winchfield, over about 9 miles of fairly level track, after which a series of signal checks stopped any further speeding. Over the un-checked sections, the 11.9 miles from Wimbledon to Weybridge were run in 10 minutes exactly, and the 6.8 miles from Farnborough to Winchfield in 5 min. 25 sec. While one cannot altogether commend harebrained running of this description—the driver evidently was in search of one of those records of which my colleague Mr. Townroe has written— the performance was at least a tribute to the exceptional powers of an engine of such relatively moderate dimensions as a " West Country " Pacific.

CHAPTER TEN

THE BULLEID PACIFICS
IN THE
INTERCHANGE TRIALS

T HE limelight which had played around the Bulleid Pacifics was further intensified in 1948, when the locomotive authorities of the newly-formed Railway Executive decided to institute comparative trials between the principal express passenger, mixed traffic, and freight classes of the four Regions. The engines selected to represent the Southern Region were, of course, the " Merchant Navy " Pacifics in the express passenger category and the " West Country " Pacifics in the mixed traffic category. While the former were meeting equals, the latter were considerably more powerful than their 4-6-0 rivals—the L.M.R. Class " 5s," the E.R. " B1s " and the W.R. " Halls." But few observers would have forecast the overwhelming superiority in performance over the 4-6-0 engines that the " West Country " Pacifics were destined to display.

Yet the Southerners were confident that, barring mechanical failures, their Pacifics would distinguish themselves. They were pleased to feel that, although the Southern had been the smallest of the four groups before nationalisation, and had spent more on electrification than upon steam locomotive development, they had locomotives capable of giving the other Regions a run for their money.

At the end of the war, a vigorous drive for improved timekeeping had been set in motion on the Southern Railway and by 1948 a very high percentage of right time arrivals was being recorded. With the intensive service of suburban trains operated by the Southern in the outer London area, any late running can have serious repercussions. It is especially important, therefore, that steam trains running into or out of the electrified area should keep to their timetable pathways, and Southern enginemen had not failed to play their part in the timekeeping drive. It is not surprising, therefore, that in the Interchange Trials Southern drivers made every effort to regain time lost by signal checks, speed restrictions or station delays, by performances which might otherwise have been regarded as in the nature of " stunting," and in this way they found numerous opportunities for displaying the capabilities of their engines. During trials over the Southern main line between Waterloo and Exeter, however, there was comparative freedom from checks, and, with the assistance of Southern pilotmen or conductors who kept an eye on their watches, the running of all the engines was more uniform, and, in general, more spirited than that elsewhere.

The Southern " Away Team," which handled the " Merchant Navy " and " West Country " Pacifics on the other Regions (with the exception of the Plymouth-Bristol runs), consisted of Driver J. Swain and Fireman A. Hooker, and Driver G. James and

Fireman G. Reynolds, all of Nine Elms Depot, with Inspector Dan Knight of the S.R. Western Division. Driver J. Swain and his mate, who performed in the Perth-Inverness trials with No. 34004 *Yeovil*, had to get their engine to and from Scotland, and in the down direction piloted express trains from Euston to Crewe and Crewe to Perth to avoid light running. In the reverse direction, however, they worked a heavy express from Perth over Beattock summit down to Carlisle without any assistance. By driving and firing over the entire 568½ miles between Euston and Inverness, Driver Swain and Fireman Hooker can claim an experience which probably is shared by no other enginemen, even on the L.M.R. or its predecessors.

Whatever official " briefing " the Southern enginemen did or did not receive, they did not lack unofficial warnings of the difficulties to come. Druimuachdar Summit would certainly be under snow ; the Highland men opened their sand valves passing Stanley Junction and kept them open all the way to Slochd Summit (incidentally, the supply of sand on a Southern Pacific was known to last for about fifteen minutes with the sand gear in full operation !) ; Carlisle, of course, was located somewhere near John o' Groats, and on the last lap of the down journey lay Shap, a railway Matterhorn, guaranteed to stall engines with dirty fires. Such warnings were lost on the Nine Elms men, however, for they were used to running the 220-odd-mile round trip from Waterloo to Bournemouth West and back without cleaning fires (unless the coal happened to be some of the Fuel Ministry's " Best Incombustible " grade), and the Euston-Carlisle run was only 80 miles longer than this. The only fear was the possibility of some slipping on the heavier gradients.

Three " Merchant Navy " engines, No. 35017 *Belgian Marine*, No. 35019 *French Line C.G.T.* and No. 35020 *Bibby Line*, were selected, and fitted with L.M.R. tenders with water-pick-up apparatus ; No. 35020 was prepared but eventually was not required to participate. Of the " West Country " type also three engines, No. 34004 *Yeovil*, No. 34005 *Barnstaple*, and No. 34006 *Bude*, were picked and equipped with L.M.R. tenders, and No. 34004 was fitted at Perth in addition with tablet-catching apparatus for use over the single-track sections of the Highland main line between Perth and Inverness. No. 35018 *British India Line* was the " Merchant Navy " Pacific used over the home ground between Waterloo and Exeter.

Although the timings of most of the test trains were easy enough, the loadings made the tasks set the engines fairly exacting. The trains, nominal tare loads and Southern engines actually used over each route, were as shown in Table 8. The loads shown were in all cases the limits, and some of the test trains were not made up to their full agreed tonnages.

The actual performances during the comparative trials have been described in full in *The Locomotive Exchanges*, 1870-1948,* and there is therefore no need to do anything more than to draw attention to some of the more spectacular achievements of the Southern engines. As none of the test trains had any very fast timings, the most outstanding feats were those uphill ; moreover, the Southern crews were not content merely to regain time that had been lost by circumstances outside their own control, but on a number of occasions ran well before time as well. Though this abounding energy with little doubt helped unduly to increase the coal consumption, those of us who are interested in performance would have been sorry indeed to have missed the opportunity of setting these striking feats on record.

On the Western Region, the best effort of " Merchant Navy " 4-6-2 No. 35019 was

---

* *By Cecil J. Allen. Ian Allan Ltd., 1949, price 15s.*

probably that of bringing a 525-ton train (492 tons tare, and 452 tons after the Reading coach had been slipped) from Westbury to Paddington, 95.6 miles, in 105 min. 10 sec., notwithstanding a 24 m.p.h. signal check at Kintbury, the Reading slack, and a permanent way slowing at Twyford ; the timetable allowed 113 minutes. In the reverse direction, a notable performance was on one of the starts from Taunton, when with 505 tons the same engine cleared Whiteball summit, 10.9 miles, in 17 min. 18 sec. As already mentioned in Chapter 6, the engine suffered from severe slipping trouble on the extremely steep gradients of South Devon, but with due allowance for out-of-course delays, even over this section net running times were within those scheduled.

The Eastern Region trains also gave No. 35017 no difficulty. Some of the uphill performances were excellent, as, for example, that of May 25th, when *Belgian Marine*, with 535 tons behind the tender, ran the 23.7 miles from Peterborough start to Stoke Summit in 28 min. 26 sec., with a fall in speed only from 55 to 50 m.p.h. up the final 3-mile ascent at 1 in 178. In the reverse direction, a notable feat of the same engine was to start a 535-ton train from Grantham up the 1 in 200 to Stoke, and, without an atom of slip, to attain 47½ m.p.h. on this grade, passing the summit box, 5.4 miles after starting, in 9 min. 37 sec.—a time for which I can find few parallels with similarly-loaded L.N.E.R. Pacifics in the pre-war heyday of L.N.E.R speeds This required an equivalent drawbar horse-power of 1,659, but was done on 25 per cent cut-off, with 200 lb. pressure in the steam-chests.

Over the London Midland Region all the competitors were hopelessly handicapped

Table 8

REGION	TRAIN	LOAD Tons, Tare	ENGINE No.
EXPRESS PASSENGER ENGINES			
London Midland ...	10.00 a.m. Euston—Carlisle	500	35017
	12.55 p.m. Carlisle—Euston	*500	35017
Eastern	1.10 p.m. King's Cross—Leeds	512	35017
	7.50 a.m. Leeds—King's Cross	512	35017
Western	1.30 p.m. Paddington—Plymouth	†485	35019
	8.30 a.m. Plymouth—Paddington	†500	35019
Southern	10.50 a.m. Waterloo—Exeter	470	35018
	12.37 p.m. Exeter—Waterloo	470	35018
MIXED TRAFFIC ENGINES			
Eastern	10.00 a.m. Marylebone—Manchester	373	34006
	8.25 a.m. Manchester—Marylebone	373	34006
London Midland ...	10.15 a.m. St. Pancras—Manchester	310	34005
	1.50 p.m. Manchester—St. Pancras	310	34005
Western	1.45 p.m. Bristol—Plymouth	‡420	34006
	1.35 p.m. Plymouth—Bristol	‡420	34006
Scottish	4.00 p.m. Perth—Inverness	§350	34004
	8.20 a.m. Inverness—Perth	§350	34004

* 474 tons Crewe—Euston.   † 360 tons between Newton Abbot and Plymouth.
‡ 275 tons between Newton Abbot and Plymouth.   § 255 tons between Aviemore and Inverness.

by permanent way and signal checks during the trials, but two momentous performances of *Belgian Marine* must be set on record. They occurred on the southbound journey, over the same stretch of track from the start at Penrith to Shap Summit. The first 3 miles of this are fairly level ; then begins the climb proper, with 7 miles right off at 1 in 125, 1¼ miles at 1 in 142, ¾-mile of level through Shap station, and a final 1¼ miles at 1 in 106-130 to Shap Summit. On the day on which I travelled *Belgian Marine* was hauling a train of 503 tons tare and 525 gross tons weight, and had been delayed by signals to Penrith, so that we started late. Getting up to 46 m.p.h. on the level start, Driver Swain then handled his engine in such a way that we settled down to an absolutely unvarying 41 m.p.h. on the 1 in 125 ; that the boiler could supply steam for an indefinite prolongation of this effort is shown by the fact that the speed rose to 46 m.p.h. on the 1 in 142 and to 51 on the short level through Shap Station ; and the final minimum at Shap Summit was 46 m.p.h. As a result, our time from Penrith to Summit, 20 min. 31 sec., cut the 27-minute schedule by no less than 6½ minutes !

It is revealed in the Official Report that this remarkable performance required an actual drawbar horsepower output of 1,540 on the 1 in 125 and 1,629 on the final 1 in 106, or equivalent drawbar horsepowers (referred to level track) of 1,860 and 1,920 respectively. The Official Report also shows that this time from Penrith to Shap Summit, with its horse-power figures, had been almost precisely duplicated by *Belgian Marine* a couple of days earlier. That the engine was far from being driven " all out " is clear from the fact that these climbs were made on 33 per cent cut-off, with the regulator nearly full open, so that, with boiler pressure maintained at just over 250 lb., there was from 215 to 225 lb. in the steam-chests.

Another notable effort, already mentioned in Chapter 6, was on the south side of Shap, when the down " Royal Scot," loaded to 530 tons, had been checked by permanent way repairs before Tebay, and so reached the foot of the final 1 in 75 ascent at no more than 57½ m.p.h. On the grade the speed had fallen to 26½ m.p.h. by Scout Green, when Swain opened out his engine to 43 per cent with full regulator, giving 255 lb. of steam in the chests as compared with 263 lb. in the boiler. As a result, the drawbar pull rose from 6.18 to 8.60 tons, and the equivalent drawbar horsepower was maintained at between 1,710 and 1,835. No other of the test competitors on the Shap climbs came anywhere near these Southern Pacific figures.

As previously indicated, however, it was the " West Country " Pacifics that achieved the major honours, and some of their achievements were quite extraordinary. The " high spots " were reached on the Great Central Section of the Eastern Region, where *Bude* was the only one of the four contestants which succeeded in keeping time, and, indeed, gaining time, with the test loads ; allowing for out-of-course checks, No. 34006 had a net gain of 14 minutes to Leicester alone on the day on which I timed the engine on the 10 a.m. from Marylebone to Manchester. Up the 1 in 105 from Rickmansworth we accelerated with 380 tons from 27 to 45 m.p.h. ; the long stretches of 1 in 176 up to Finmere and Helmdon were surmounted at minimum speeds of 61 and 64 m.p.h. respectively ; but the most extraordinary performance was an acceleration from 20 m.p.h. through Hucknall Central (the result of a permanent way check) to precisely 50 m.p.h. up the continuous 1 in 132 climb to Annesley.

The equivalent drawbar horsepower required for this performance was no less than 1,960, and for the climbing of Chalfont bank (to Amersham) 1,639 ; the former required no more than 30 per cent cut-off and the latter 25 per cent, with the regulator nearly full open (225 lb. steam-chest and 245 lb. boiler : 235 lb. steam-chest and 270 lb. boiler respectively). The most thrilling piece of running was the start-to-stop time of 31 min. 24 sec. for the 31.2 miles from Aylesbury to Woodford, largely uphill, with a top speed of 76½ m.p.h. on but little easier than level track near Quainton Road, as set out in Table 9.

In the reverse direction, the highest equivalent drawbar horsepower recorded throughout the whole of the exchange trials, with any type of locomotive (apart from one higher figure sustained for a moment or two only), was that of *Bude* after getting away from Leicester on June 11th, when the engine maintained a steady 58-57 m.p.h. up the entire length of the long 1 in 176 from Whetstone, with 395 tons of train, on 27 per cent cut-off and full regulator, keeping up 240 lb. pressure in the steam-chests and 260 lb. in the boiler ; the actual drawbar horsepower so developed was 1,667 and the equivalent figure was 2,010. Two days earlier I noted an almost unbelievable start, with the same engine and load, from Aylesbury. Less than ½-mile from the platform end there begins the 1 in 117 climb which continues, apart from ¼-mile interruptions through Stoke Mandeville and Wendover stations, for 5½ miles, followed by an easing to 1 in 132-158 for the final mile to Dutchlands summit. Here *Bude* worked up to 47½ m.p.h. before

Table 9

THE EXCHANGE TESTS, 1948

Distance	Engine : " West Country " 4-6-2 No. 34006 *Bude*. Load : 360 tons tare, 380 tons gross.					min. sec.	m.p.h.
miles						0 00	—
0·0	AYLESBURY ...	...	...	...	...	7 57	69/76½
6·2	Quainton Road	...	...	...	...	10 18	*67
8·9	Grendon Underwood Junction	...	...	...		12 04	65/71½
10·9	Calvert	...	...	...	...	17 18	59/75
16·6	Finmere	...	...	...	...	21 42	68
21·4	Brackley	...	...	...	...	24 46	64/69
24·6	Helmdon	...	...	...	...	28 01	65
28·2	Culworth	...	...	...	...	29 07	69
29·4	Culworth Junction	...	...	...		31 24	—
31·2	WOODFORD HALSE	...	...	...			
miles						min. sec.	m.p.h.
0·0	RUGBY	...	...	...	...	0 00	—
3·6	Shawell	...	...	...	...	5 03	60/61
6·8	Lutterworth	...	...	...	...	8 04	70½/61
10·7	Ashby Magna	...	...	...		11 22	75
15·2	Whetstone	...	...	...	...	15 13	eased
18·9	Leicester Goods Junction South	...	...		18 30	*62
19·9	LEICESTER	...	...	...	...	20 07	—
	Load : 449 tons tare, 475 tons gross.						
miles						min. sec.	m.p.h.
0·0	TAUNTON	...	...	...	...	0 00	—
2·4	Creech Junction	...	...	...		4 20	55
5·8	Durston	...	...	...	...	7 32	70½
11·6	BRIDGWATER	...	...	...		12 23	72
14·1	Dunball	...	...	...	...	14 28	73
17·9	HIGHBRIDGE	...	...	...		17 37	72
20·6	Brent Knoll	...	...	...		20 00	66½
25·1	Uphill Junction	...	...	...		24 06	64
28·0	Worle Junction	...	...	...		26 42	70
32·8	YATTON	...	...	...	...	30 46	74
36·7	Nailsea	...	...	...	...	33 56	75
38·9	Flax Bourton	...	...	...		35 49	70
41·6	Long Ashton	...	...	...		37 59	75
						Sig. stop	
44·8	BRISTOL (T.M.)	...	...	...		47 59	—

* Speed restriction.

Wendover, accelerated to 50 through the station, settled down to 48 on the rest of the 1 in 117, and went over the summit at 51 ! Once again the cut-off was 27 per cent and the regulator wide open ; the drawbar horsepowers so developed were 1,416 actual and 1,777 equivalent.

As with the " Merchant Navy " Pacific, the " West Country " 4-6-2 broke no records on the tremendous banks of the Western Region between Newton Abbot and Plymouth, where fear of slipping doubtless counselled caution. But Driver Snell made one brilliant run with *Bude* from Taunton to Bristol on July 21st, demonstrating the ability of a " West Country " boiler to supply steam for the maintenance of more than 70 m.p.h. for miles on end of a level course with a gross load of 475 tons. About 2½ miles after starting the engine was doing a mile-a-minute, and in 6 miles speed had risen to over 70, after which it continued at between 70 and 75 until steam was shut off for the approach to Bristol 36 miles later. The average speed over 35.8 miles from Durston to Long Ashton was 70.5 m.p.h., and the latter station, 41.6 miles from the Taunton start, was passed in 37 min. 59 sec., a glorious sprint indeed. This also appears in Table 8.

Up in the Highlands the performances of *Yeovil*, the first Pacific locomotive ever to run over the Highland main line, were outstanding and at times positively amusing. The " star turn " was on July 13th, when *Yeovil* got away from Blair Atholl with such vigour as to " wind " the banker, ex-Caledonian 4-4-0 No. 14501, so that the re-start from Struan had to be delayed while the assistant was piling on a little more steam ! When the train set to work on the great 1 in 70 climb from Struan, the Southern 4-6-2 settled down to an average speed of 36.3 m.p.h., putting out an average of 1,115 horsepower at the drawbar for 10 miles continuously, with no more than 25 per cent cut-off and practically full regulator. So the two engines between them lifted their 380-ton train up the 11.3 miles from Struan to Dalnaspidal in 19 min. 23 sec., some 11½ minutes less than the 31 minutes allowed by the timetable !

Other high power outputs were developed by *Yeovil* in climbing from Dalwhinnie start to the summit at Druimuachdar, where on July 14th the engine was exerting an actual drawbar horsepower averaging 1,377 for five minutes continuously, on 30 per cent cut-off ; the maximum equivalent drawbar horsepowers over this stage on July 14th and 16th were 1,912 and 1,950 respectively, the latter with 35 per cent cut-off, up a 1 in 80 gradient. Further north, also, the even steeper starts out of Inverness, with many miles up at 1 in 60, were tackled successfully with a lighter load of 260 tons ; from 25 to 27 m.p.h. was sustained up this grade, with a recovery to 33½ on the succeeding 1 in 70 and a quick speed-up to 50 across Culloden Moor viaduct ; 28 m.p.h. was the minimum on the next 1 in 60 stretch, so that 6¾ minutes had been gained in the first 10.8 miles to Daviot, which occupied 21 min. 15 sec.

So the catalogue might be continued, but enough has been written to show that the boilers of the Southern Pacifics, both the heavy and the light, can supply steam in ample volume to meet the most exacting demands ; even in the achievement of feats of perform-ance that were of considerable note, cut-offs of 25 to 33 per cent would hardly indicate that the engines were being " extended " to secure such results. That is to say, they were working well within capacity in responding to every demand made on them by the heaviest loads and steepest gradients of the test routes. These maximum feats must be seen in their perspective, of course. Though the Southern Pacifics achieved the record horsepower outputs of the trials, considerably higher outputs have been registered by E.R. Pacifics of the " A4 " type and L.M.R. " Duchess " Pacifics on other test occasions ; one of the latter, indeed, has scored a British record of 2,511 equivalent drawbar horsepower.

It is also necessary to add that the efficiency figures during the trials were considerably less flattering to the Bulleid Pacifics. With one single exception, their coal and water consumptions were higher than those of any other express passenger or mixed traffic class of locomotive that was included in the exchanges, as may be seen in Table 10. On the other hand, as shown in Table 11, they were near the top of the table when it came to boiler efficiency, as measured by the evaporation rate. It would thus appear that what was being gained in boiler efficiency was being lost by a considerably lower standard of efficiency in the use of steam at the front end. No doubt the working of the engines over

Table 10

THE 1948 EXCHANGES

AVERAGE CONSUMPTIONS RELATED TO POWER OUTPUT

COAL		WATER	
Locomotive	lb. per drawbar—h.p.-hour	Locomotive	lb. per drawbar—h.p.-hour
E.R. " A4 " 4-6-2	3·06	E.R. " A4 " 4-6-2	24·32
L.M.R. " Duchess " 4-6-2	3·12	L.M.R. " Royal Scot " 4-6-0	25·81
L.M.R. " Royal Scot " 4-6-0	3·38	L.M.R. " Duchess " 4-6-2	27·08
L.M.R. Class " 5 " 4-6-0	3·54	E.R. " B1 " 4-6-0	27·64
W.R. " King " 4-6-0	3·59*	L.M.R. Class " 5 " 4-6-0	27·99
E.R. " B1 " 4-6-0	3·57	W.R. " King " 4-6-0	28·58‡
S.R. " Merchant Navy " 4-6-2	3·60	W.R. " Hall " 4-6-0	29·97§
W.R. " Hall " 4-6-0	3·94†	S.R. " Merchant Navy " 4-6-2	30·43
S.R. " West Country " 4-6-2	4·11	S.R. " West Country " 4-6-2	32·64

Additional tests of W.R. engines with Welsh coal :

* Standard " King," 3·33 lb. ; high superheat " King," 3·10 lb.   † " Hall," 3·22 lb.

‡ Standard " King," 30·46 lb. ; high superheat " King," 27·47 lb.   § " Hall," 31·68 lb.

long stretches of line with a relatively small regulator opening would help to account in part for loss of efficiency, by throttling of the steam ; imperceptible slipping, as revealed on Rattery bank of the Western Region and elsewhere, might also account for loss of power ; but the front end design cannot be acquitted of all responsibility. To what extent the difference in driving method adopted by the Southern enginemen, as compared with the caution of most of their colleagues, affected the efficiency figures, it is difficult to pronounce with any certainty.

As already mentioned, the pronounced tendency of these engines to slip, even when running at speed, came under adverse comment in the Official Report, and can hardly fail to escape the notice of any observer who watches a Southern Pacific starting away from a stop. This tendency may be attributed to a number of technical causes other than the high power-weight ratio, with its resultant low factor of

Table 11

THE 1948 EXCHANGES
AVERAGE BOILER EVAPORATION RATES

Locomotive	lb. of water per lb. of coal
L.M.R. " Duchess " 4-6-2	8·67
S.R. " Merchant Navy " 4-6-2	8·45
W.R. " King " 4-6-0	8·07*
S.R. " West Country " 4-6-2	7·94
E.R. " A4 " 4-6-2	7·92
L.M.R. Class " 5 " 4-6-0	7·92
L.M.R. " Royal Scot " 4-6-0	7·70
W.R. " Hall " 4-6-0	7·69†
E.R. " B1 " 4-6-0	7·68

Additional tests of W.R. engines with Welsh coal :
* Standard " King," 9·15 lb. ; high superheat " King," 8·86 lb.
† " Hall," 9·84 lb.

adhesion, though the 3.76 adhesion factor of a " Merchant Navy " 4-6-2 and the 4.06 of a " West Country " actually are no lower than the 3.75 of a Western " King " or a London Midland " Duchess." But the Southern regulator uses no pilot valve, and superheater, steam-pipes and steam-chests hold a considerable volume of steam, so that slipping on starting is difficult to control without the most scrupulously careful handling ; also the steam sanding is not entirely satisfactory, as the sand-traps and pipes tend to become clogged with oil from the oil-bath. The latter handicap, however, would not account for the slipping at speed.

CHAPTER ELEVEN

OPERATING PROBLEMS AND LOCOMOTIVE DEVELOPMENT

No study of the Bulleid Pacifics would be complete without reference to the exceptional interest—amounting at times to violent partisanship—which these engines have aroused amongst all followers of locomotive practice. Wherever technicians, footplate men or knowledgeable amateurs have gathered together, sooner or later the conversation has turned to praise or criticism of them. In the long history of the steam locomotive in this country, it is doubtful if any other design has stirred up quite so much debate. The disputants have aired their views in print, by articles and correspondence, in such diverse journals as *The Railway Gazette*, *The Railway Magazine*, *Trains Illustrated*, *The Model Engineer* and *The Locomotive Express*. In the pages of the last-named, which circulates mainly amongst the footplate staff of British Railways, Southern drivers and firemen have come forward strongly in defence of the capabilities of their Pacifics.

The consensus of opinion amongst the enginemen, who are in a good position to judge, has been that the engines, when in good condition, display complete mastery of their work, and are capable of running their trains to time, in all possible conditions of road, load and schedule, as is supported by the facts and figures in the preceding chapters. Criticisms by drivers have centred mainly in the poor visibility from the footplate and the difficulty of diagnosing internal defects. On more than one occasion the total enclosure of motion has proved an embarrassment to enginemen, who have had to incur delay in sending for a replacement engine because of a defect which, with exposed motion, could have been put right in a few moments. At times British locomotive lovers have scorned foreign locomotives for having " everything but a kitchen stove " festooning their exteriors, but the opposite condition, where everything is boxed in, can be most tantalising when the source of a slight steam or oil leak requires the removal of several sheets of steel casing before it can be traced. This lack of accessibility is equally a source of complaint in the engine-sheds, and undoubtedly has tended to increase the costs of maintenance.

In order to meet these and other difficulties connected with handling and maintenance which have arisen since the Bulleid Pacifics first went into service, various modifications of the design have been made, the most noticeable externally being the changes aimed at improving the look-out ahead. One of the worst troubles has been the blanketing of the cab front windows by drifting exhaust. This nuisance is not experienced with locomotives whose chimneys stand well proud of the smokebox, as, for example, those of the Western Region, but on the Bulleid Pacifics the boiler casing was carried right up to the loading gauge, and the chimney top had, therefore, to be flush with the top of the casing. At the same time, in order to preserve unrestricted access to the smokebox door, and to avoid the inconvenience and the extra weight of a sloping front, as used on the L.N.E.R. and the L.M.S.R. streamlined Pacifics, the front of the Bulleid Pacific was arranged to present a vertical, flat surface to the air, and the shape of the engine was therefore not truly streamlined, but only " air-smoothed."

The first ten " Merchant Navy " engines were designed with the front as shown in the illustrations on pages 18 (upper) and 21 (upper). By providing an air channel over the top of the smokebox and around the chimney, it was hoped that air would flow up over the top of the engine, carrying smoke and steam with it. But the results were unsatisfactory, even with the enlarged air channel seen on page 65 (top right). Wind-tunnel tests were then conducted at University College, Southampton, with the aid of a one-inch scale model, using vaporised paraffin to simulate white smoke from the chimney. These tests demonstrated that air disturbance caused by the flat front could be minimised by leading the frontal air round the corners of the smokebox, using curved plates for the purpose. An arrangement of this kind was fitted full size to No. 21C10 *Blue Star*, as shown on page 65 (centre), and experiments were tried also on No. 21C8 *Orient Line* and No. 21C9 *Shaw Savill*. Observers rode on these locomotives, and records of the behaviour of the smoke and steam at speed were secured by mounting a cinematograph camera behind the cab front window on the driver's side.

The arrangement on *Blue Star* gave very good results, but it increased the width of the smokebox front and thus reduced the enginemen's view. A compromise was reached, however, by making the side screens flat, similar to the well-tried deflector screens. The driver could then see between the screen and the side of the smokebox ; in other words, the only obstruction was the actual thickness of the screen itself. A curved cowling across the top front edge of the smokebox was retained, but it was made separate from the side screens, and the revised front end, seen on page 65 (bottom), was fitted to the first twenty " Merchant Navy " engines. But the vagaries of the weather and its influence on the behaviour of the smoke and steam showed that even yet the ideal solution had not been reached. The least favourable conditions occur in damp misty weather, when steam condenses rapidly and hangs round the engine, and also, as is almost inevitable with an engine of the size and shape of the prototype under discussion, in certain wind conditions when a side wind causes a low pressure area on the leeward side of the engine. The position of signals is another factor ; signals fixed directly over the track on gantries, a common practice on the Southern Region, obviously are more liable to be obscured by smoke and steam than those standing at the lineside.

In spite of the improvement secured by the arrangement shown at the bottom of page 65, therefore, it left something to be desired in poor weather conditions, and the investigation was resumed. Various engines were fitted with additional lengths of side screening, extended towards the cab. Screens with frontal curvature, on the same principle as those applied to No. 21C10 but on a smaller scale, were temporarily fitted to Engine 21C162, as seen on page 70. While these experiments were in progress, engines could be observed with gay decorations consisting of tassels of coloured string attached to the side screens, but their purpose was not festive, for they were being used to observe the direction of air currents. A longer length of side screen was finally standardised.

Attention was then focused on the footplate end of the engine, and by changing the flat-fronted to a V-fronted cab it was possible to increase the size of the cab front windows, and to bring the driver's window closer to him. The windows can be easily reached, for cleaning purposes, from the side apertures. As yet the V-fronted cab has not been applied to all the Pacifics. It should, perhaps, be emphasised that occasional interference with the driver's vision, by steam and smoke, is almost impossible to prevent, and afflicts many engines other than those under discussion. This fact does not imply any lack of safety, because a driver possesses an intimate acquaintance with the position of all signals, and if necessary can shut off steam and apply the blower if there is any likelihood of interference with the reading of signal indications. Moreover, both sides of the engine are not affected simultaneously. The ideal solution would be to place the cab in front of the engine, but this is difficult unless firing is with fuel oil which can be piped from the tender to a firebox at the front end, as in the well-known Southern Pacific 4-8-8-2 cab-in-front locomotives in the U.S.A.

The general appearance of the Bulleid Pacifics is admired by some, and disliked by others, according to personal aesthetic taste. At anyrate, a far neater outline has been achieved than has been the case with some of the world's streamlined designs which have undergone similar post-constructional alterations to improve the smoke deflection. A study of the streamlined locomotives produced in France, Belgium, Germany, the United States and Japan between 1930 and 1940 leaves the honours easily with the Bulleid Pacifics by comparison with most of them !

Other critics, with an eye to maintenance problems, have contended that the brilliance of the performance of the Bulleid Pacifics has not been consistent, and that in addition to the high fuel, water and oil consumption of the engines, their availability, in day-to-day service, has fallen short of the standard set by more conventional and reliable locomotives. It cannot be disputed that there have been difficulties in maintenance, and some of these now require examination. Bearing in mind the tremendous handicap of Southern Region weight limits, discussed in Chapter 1, and the war and post-war shortage of certain materials, it is not altogether surprising that some details have shown weakness. The price of weight reduction has had to be paid, in the lack of a sufficient margin of strength in certain parts to meet higher power output demands.

Breakage of main frames of the Bulleid Pacifics, for example, recalls the difficulties with Drummond's early four-cylinder engines, which did not have the cylinders in line, and suffered from inadequate bracing of the frames. This particular trouble, connected with the flexure of the frames, has been under investigation, and No. 34039 *Boscastle* has been fitted with an indicator shelter at the front end, to enable measurements of frame movements to be recorded. A similar shelter can be seen on page 41, mounted on No. 34005. In the past, one simple remedy for broken parts has been to increase their strength, regardless of corresponding weight increases, but when total weights approach a given limit, then the designer is compelled to find a new way to circumvent the obstacles in his path. Experiments have also been proceeding, for example, with the development of corrugated steam and exhaust pipes, of thinner and lighter material than the pipes usually employed.

Another contentious point about the Bulleid Pacifics, round which unending discussion has raged, is their unique chain-driven valve-motion. Critics have claimed that the irregular beats which develop in some of the engines after a lengthy period out of the

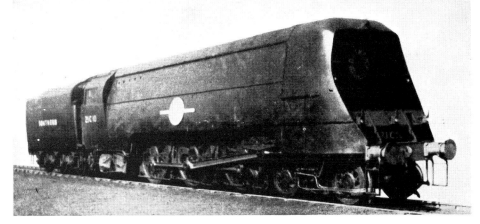

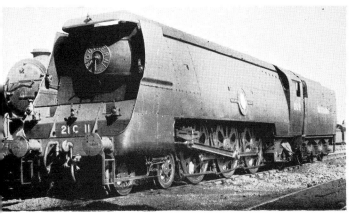

After wind tunnel experiments at University College, Southampton, a new front end was devised for No. 21C10 early in 1943 (*above*) and fitted later to No. 21C8. No. 21C11 (*left*) illustrates the final outcome of these first experiments, with the upper part of the new side shield separated from the main body. Note the rounded casing enclosing the outside cylinder, now removed.

[*British Railways, M. W. Earley*

SMOKE DEFLECTION—" Merchant Navy " No. 21C5 *Canadian Pacific* (*above*) illustrates the first series after the front had been modified to accord with the new pattern smoke deflector design. The train is the up " Atlantic Coast Express," near Honiton. The final pattern of " Merchant Navy " deflection is seen (*below*) on No. 35026 (unnamed), heading an up Weymouth express on Parkstone bank, Dorset, June 10th, 1949. Note the light Pacific tender with which some engines of the third series first appeared, before their 6,000 gallon tenders were ready.   [*W. N. Lockett, H. Weston*

SMOKE DEFLECTION—To-day, the deflectors of the first series of " Merchant Navies " are longer, compared with those seen at the top of the previous page, to accord with those on the last two series ; note also the rebuilt cab, compared with the picture on page 19. No. 35008 *Orient Line* is at speed near Winchfield with the 12.50 p.m. Waterloo-West of England express in May, 1950.

[*M.W. Earley*]

SMOKE DEFLECTION—Extra-length deflectors were at one time fitted to some Pacifics, among them "Merchant Navy" No. 35020 *Bibby Line*, seen passing Woking with the down "Bournemouth Belle" on January 15th, 1949.

[*G. I. Jefferson*

SMOKE DEFLECTION—Evidence of the attention demanded by the problem is provided by this picture of "West Country" No. 21C119 (unnamed) near Ashford with the down "Golden Arrow" (*above*), before lengthening of the deflectors. No. 34006 *Bude*, leaving Exeter St. Davids with a Plymouth train (*below*), was one light Pacific to be fitted with extra-length deflectors. [*P. Ransome-Wallis, J. P. Wilson*

SMOKE DEFLECTI▪
In 1947 the deflec▪
of light Pacific ▪
21C162 (*left*) w▪
turned inward exp▪
mentally. The eng▪
heads   a   Lond▪
Ramsgate express ▪
Knockholt. The p▪
sent standard deflec▪
length is illustrated ▪
No.   21C140   (▪
addition   is   clea▪
visible),   heading ▪
down "Golden Arro▪
out of Victoria (*belo*▪
[*B. A. Reeves,*
Eric Tr▪

THE "DEVON BELLE"—
To avoid a public stop at
Salisbury, this train, introduced in 1947, changes
engines at Wilton. "Mer-
chant Navy" No. 21C10
Blue Star relieves No. 21C14
Nederland Line on the westbound train (*above*). For a
short while after its in-
auguration the up Ilfra-
combe portion was both
piloted and banked up the
1 in 36 gradient to Mortehoe
by "West Country"
Pacifics, of which No.
34116 *Bodmin* is providing
rear-end assistance in this
picture (*right*).

J. Jefferies, C. Todhunter

THE "THANET BELLE," largest of the Southern Pullman trains and now renamed the "Kentish Belle," near Chislehurst. "Battle of Britain"

shops, indicate that the valve-gear arrangement is not ideal. In reply it may be pointed out that the Bulleid motion is not the only valve-gear to show such characteristics ; irregular beats are by no means unknown with the most conventional of valve-gears, and with the Gresley conjugate valve-gear for three-cylinder engines over-travel of the middle cylinder ports, by over-travel of the valves, has given, as is well known, a considerable amount of trouble. But as regards the Bulleid motion, it must be conceded that, although very adequate provision has been made for lubrication, cumulative lost motion in the gear employed to operate the valves, amplified as it is by the unequal rocker arms used to step-up the travel of the valves from that of the radius rods, is inevitable, and must result in some loss of efficiency.

As to the use of chain-drive to the valve-gear, the chains themselves have given excellent service, but where very accurate phasing is required (as, for example, the chain-driven camshafts of internal combustion engines), some automatic slack adjustment is desirable. In applying chain-drive to a locomotive valve-gear, complications in chain-tensioning arise because the chain is not uni-directional, and operates in a reverse direction when the engine is in backward gear. Further, the crank axle not only rises and falls but possesses some lateral freedom of movement. There has been no stretching of the chain links, but the cumulative effect of wear on the pins and in the holes, as also of the sprocket teeth, means that the total length of the longer chain, with its 118 links, can be increased by as much as $5\frac{1}{2}$ or 6 inches between shoppings, and the consequential sag of the chain has caused external wear on some of the engines, by rubbing. Actually, breakages of chains have been rare, but the difficulty of taking up this slack—either by repositioning the intermediate sprocket cradle, or varying the thickness of liners, or taking out one or two links—is a disadvantage. In existing circumstances it is doubtful if any successful means could be devised for maintaining the correct tension of the chains automatically.

Modifications have been made to various items connected with the oil-bath, with the object of preventing oil loss by way of the radius rod spindles passing through the front of the bath, and by way of the crank axle, as well as from various joints in the construction of the oil bath itself. Splits in the metal of which the sump is fabricated, due to vibration, also have not been unknown. The scale on which oil is lost may be realised when it is mentioned that the lubricating oil consumption of a Bulleid Pacific on the average is far more than that of a " King Arthur " or " Lord Nelson " 4-6-0. Fires have originated from time to time in the firebox and boiler lagging of these engines, due to the soaking of the lagging with oil which has escaped in various ways, as mentioned in Chapter Three, and these fires at times have proved troublesome. Another difficulty has been that of water finding its way into the oil-bath, both as a result of condensation and also of leakages from steam fittings on the boiler above the bath. But there has been a slight gain in the maintenance of the inside motion due to the oil bath. It is rare for one of the Pacifics to be stopped on account of any heating of the big or small ends of the inside cylinder connecting rods. It is not unusual for one of these engines to run up to 80,000 miles without any refilling or boring of the brasses of the inside big-end, and 75 to 80 per cent. of the small ends do not need to be touched after the same mileage. Maintenance work inside the oil bath tends to be a cramped and tedious process, although this difficulty would not arise if the original intention of confining any need for such attention to general overhauls had proved to be practicable.

Several other changes are deserving of mention. Modifications were carried out, on

73

G

the early " Merchant Navy " class engines, to the cylinders. Breakage of the rocker-shaft arms was attributed to unequal steam pressure on the piston valve-heads at certain instants in the working cycle, causing excessive load to be thrown on the valve operating gear. A balance-pipe between the ends of each steam chest was incorporated in the revised design of cylinder casting. Subsequently, additional bearings were provided to support the rocker shafts, and various alterations were made to the piston-valve liners to prevent breakage of piston-valve heads.

The earlier Pacifics had sanding gear applied to the centre pair of coupled wheels only. This was extended first to the leading, and afterwards to the trailing, coupled wheels, in an attempt to cure slipping troubles. The leading sands have since been removed, owing to sand finding its way on to the working surfaces of the slidebars ; a temporary cure for this was sought by fitting covers over the slidebars on many engines, but without complete success. The position of the sand-boxes high up under the boiler casing, with filling holes that can only be reached by ladders, no doubt was dictated by the general arrangement of the rest of the engine, but is far from ideal. Clogging of the sand-pipes with oil from the sump is difficult to deal with owing to their inaccessibility. Easy cleaning of the boiler casing also is not easy in the absence of running-boards. Like the sand-boxes, the mechanical lubricators are not ideally placed ; they are located in front of and below the smokebox, where, in normal operating conditions, the daily process of clearing the smoke-box of ashes inevitably conflicts with the necessity to preserve scrupulous cleanliness where lubrication is concerned.

The provision of a steam reverser is a matter of individual preference, but unless the engine requires reversing repeatedly, as in shunting, the screw-reverser is generally preferred by drivers. The latter is certainly more positive and allows much finer adjustments of cut-off, by feel and not sight, than a steam-reverser.

The boilers of the Bulleid Pacifics, as Chapters 6 to 10 have demonstrated in no uncertain fashion, have been their most outstanding asset. Notable assistance to firebox circulation and to steaming is given by the thermic syphons, and with careful maintenance and servicing of the firebox, the welding of junctions between syphons and firebox walls and of the firebox generally has given little trouble. In order to avoid cracks in plates resulting from excessive contraction, one essential is that a Pacific shall be allowed to stand for some twelve hours after coming into the shed, before boiler washing out begins, if cold water is to be used ; another necessary procedure is to clean out the ash thoroughly from the combustion chamber at the firebox end of the barrel. A valuable contribution to reduced boiler maintenance costs has been the fitting of the French " T.I.A." water treatment apparatus to the tenders of the Pacifics ; with this in use, provided the boiler is blown down twice on each daily run, the period between boiler washings-out has been extended to 56 days.

In concluding this book, the authors would state that their endeavour has been to enable the reader to obtain a more balanced view of these contentious locomotives than may be possible from reading the partisan views of their protagonists or their critics, as set forth in the technical press, or from listening to the rumours that circulate concerning them, often wildly exaggerated. Chapter 2 has explained that there were well thought-out reasons behind all the departures from the traditional in design, and the only criticism that might be ventured in the realm is that a more lengthy period of trial, with a limited number of engines, would have been desirable before these features became incorporated in a total of 140 locomotives. If in some respects these engines have proved disappointing, however, it must be remembered that many of their features have proved singularly successful, and many diseases which plague older types of locomotives have been almost eliminated, such as heated axleboxes, hot inside big-ends, broken spokes and loose tyres, leaky valve-spindles, expanded and leaky tube-plates, wasted firebox lap joints, and so on. Thus it is hardly surprising that some of the better features of the Bulleid Pacifics have found their way into British Railways standard designs. Any profit and loss account must also take into consideration the undoubted value of experimentation.

Where do we go from here ? If Isambard Kingdom Brunel of the Great Western had had his way with the Broad Gauge, it might not be so difficult for locomotive designers to-day to find the answer ! But the designer nowadays is like a juggler, striving to balance strength against weight and size, and performance against simplicity and low costs. One school of thought tends toward utter simplicity as the practical answer for the reduction of maintenance costs and the achievement of great reliability ; indeed, a reversion to simplicity often has followed past tendencies towards complication on the part of individual designers. General working conditions in the industry have since made such progress, however, that a policy of " Simplicity First " is unlikely to prove desirable in recruiting suitable or even sufficient staff to handle and maintain steam locomotives in future, if thereby the steam engine remains a dirty and unattractive machine, the poor relation of the electric and the diesel locomotive. Fortunately there are signs that with various modern developments much can yet be done to satisfy the conflicting views of designers, manufacturers and operators.

The Chief Mechanical and Electrical Engineer of the Railway Executive, Mr. R. A. Riddles, in his address to the Institution of Locomotive Engineers of November, 1950, pointed out, in presenting the case for the steam locomotive, that both in first cost and actual fuel costs per unit of power at the drawbar the steam engine is still more than holding its own, on an economic basis, with competitive forms of motive power. Such a considered view as this is heartening. Moreover, whatever may be the views expressed either for or against the Bulleid Pacifics, it must be agreed that they have contributed in no small measure to the locomotive knowledge that will help to assure a future for steam traction on railways.

APPENDIX A

THE BULLEID PACIFICS—PRINCIPAL DIMENSIONS

	"MERCHANT NAVY"	"WEST COUNTRY" and "BATTLE OF BRITAIN"
Cylinders (3) diameter	18 in.	16⅜ in.
,, stroke	24 in.	24 in.
Coupled wheels, diameter	6 ft. 2 in.	6 ft. 2 in.
Bogie ,, ,, ...	3 ft. 1 in.	3 ft. 1 in.
Trailing ,, ,, ...	3 ft. 7 in.	3 ft. 1 in.
Wheelbase, coupled	15 ft. 0 in.	14 ft. 9 in.
,, total engine	36 ft. 9 in.	35 ft. 6 in.
Heating surface : Firebox and siphons	275 sq. ft.	253 sq. ft.
Tubes and flues	2,176 ,,	1,869 ,,
Total evaporative	2,451 ,,	2,122 ,,
Superheating surface	822 ,,	545 ,,
Combined heating surfaces	3,273 ,,	2,667 ,,
Firegate area	48.5 ,,	38.25 ,,
Working pressure (per sq. in.)	280 lb.	280 lb.
Adhesion weight	63.0 tons	56.25 tons
Weight of engine in working order	94.75 ,,	86.0 ,,
Coal capacity of tender	5 tons	5 tons
Water capacity of tender	⎰ 5,000 gal.*† ⎱ 6,000 ,, ‡	4,500 gal.§ 5,500 ,, ¶
Weight of tender, full	⎧ 47,80 tons * ⎨ 49.35 ,, † ⎩ 53.30 ,, ‡	⎱ 42.6 tons§ ⎰ 47.25 ,, ¶
Total weight, engine and tender	⎧ 142.55 tons * ⎨ 144.1 ,, † ⎩ 148.05 ,, ‡	⎱ 128.6 tons § ⎰ 133.25 ,, ¶
Max. width of engine	9 ft. 0 in.	8 ft. 6 in.
,, height ,, ...	12 ft. 11 in.	12 ft. 11 in.
Tractive effort (at 85 per cent working pressure) ..	37,500 lb.	31,000 lb.

*Nos. 35001-10   †Nos. 35011-20   ‡Nos. 35021-30   §Nos. 34001-70/91-110   ¶Nos. 34071-90

APPENDIX B

NUMBERS, NAMES AND BUILDING DATES
"MERCHANT NAVY" CLASS

NO.	NAME	DATE NEW	NO.	NAME	DATE NEW
35001	*Channel Packet*	2/41	35016	*Elders Fyffes*	3/45
35002	*Union Castle*	6/41	35017	*Belgian Marine*	4/45
35003	*Royal Mail*	9/41	35018	*British India Line*	5/45
35004	*Cunard White Star* ..	10/41	35019	*French Line C.G.T.*	6/45
35005	*Canadian Pacific*	12/41	35020	*Bibby Line*	6/45
35006	*Peninsula and Oriental S. N. Co.*	12/41	35021	*New Zealand Line*	9/48
35007	*Aberdeen Commonwealth* ..	6/42	35022	*Holland America Line* ..	10/48
35008	*Orient Line*	6/42	35023	*Holland-Afrika Line* ..	11/48
35009	*Shaw Savill*	7/42	35024	*East Asiatic Company* ..	11/48
35010	*Blue Star*	8/42	35025	*Brocklebank Line*	11/48
35011	*General Steam Navigation* ..	12/44	35026	*Lamport & Holt Line* ..	12/48
35012	*United States Line*	12/44	35027	*Port Line*	12/48
35013	*Blue Funnel*	2/45	35028	*Clan Line*	12/48
35014	*Nederland Line*	2/45	35029	*Ellerman Lines*	2/49
35015	*Rotterdam Lloyd*	3/45	35030	*Elder-Dempster Lines* ..	4/49

"WEST COUNTRY" AND "BATTLE OF BRITAIN" CLASSES

NOTE : Not all these locomotives have received their nameplates at the time of writing.

NO.	NAME	DATE	NO.	NAME	DATE
34001	Exeter	6/45	34056	Croydon	2/47
34002	Salisbury	6/45	34057	Biggin Hill	3/47
34003	Plymouth	6/45	34058	Sir Frederick Pile	4/47
34004	Yeovil	7/45	34059	Sir Archibald Sinclair	4/47
34005	Barnstaple	7/45	34060	25 Squadron	4/47
34006	Bude	8/45	34061	73 Squadron	4/47
34007	Wadebridge	9/45	34062	17 Squadron	5/47
34008	Padstow	9/45	34063	229 Squadron	5/47
34009	Lyme Regis	9/45	34064	Fighter Command	7/47
34010	Sidmouth	9/45	34065	Hurricane	7/47
34011	Tavistock	10/45	34066	Spitfire	9/47
34012	Launceston	10/45	34067	Tangmere	9/47
34013	Okehampton	10/45	34068	Kenley	10/47
34014	Budleigh Salterton	11/45	34069	Hawkinge	10/47
34015	Exmouth	11/45	34070	Manston	10/47
34016	Bodmin	11/45	34071	601 Squadron	4/48
34017	Ilfracombe	12/45	34072	257 Squadron	4/48
34018	Axminster	12/45	34073	249 Squadron	5/48
34019	Bideford	12/45	34074	46 Squadron	5/48
34020	Seaton	12/45	34075	264 Squadron	6/48
34021	Dartmoor	1/46	34076	41 Squadron	6/48
34022	Exmoor	1/46	34077	603 Squadron	7/48
34023	Blackmore Vale	2/46	34078	222 Squadron	7/48
34024	Tamar Valley	2/46	34079	141 Squadron	7/48
34025	Whimple	3/46	34080	74 Squadron	8/48
34026	Yes Tor	4/46	34081	92 Squadron	9/48
34027	Taw Valley	4/46	34082	615 Squadron	9/48
34028	Eddystone	5/46	34083	605 Squadron	10/48
34029	Lundy	5/46	34084	253 Squadron	11/48
34030	Watersmeet	5/46	34085	501 Squadron	11/48
34031	Torrington	6/46	34086	219 Squadron	12/48
34032	Camelford	6/46	34087	145 Squadron	12/48
34033	Chard	6/46	34088	213 Squadron	12/48
34034	Honiton	7/46	34089	602 Squadron	12/48
34035	Shaftesbury	7/46	34090	Sir Eustace Missenden Southern	
34036	Westward Ho !	7/46		Railway	2/49
34037	Clovelly	8/46	34091	Weymouth	9/49
34038	Lynton	9/46	34092	City of Wells*	9/49
34039	Boscastle	9/46	34093	Saunton	9/49
34040	Crewkerne	9/46	34094	Mortehoe	10/49
34041	Wilton	9/46	34095	Brentor	10/49
34042	Dorchester	10/46	34096	Trevone	11/49
34043	Combe Martin	10/46	34097	Holsworthy	11/49
34044	Woolacombe	10/46	34098	Templecombe	12/49
34045	Ottery St. Mary	10/46	34099	Lynmouth	12/49
34046	Braunton	11/46	34100	Appledore	12/49
34047	Callington	11/46	34101	Hartland	1/50
34048	Crediton	11/46	34102	Lapford	2/50
34049	Anti-Aircraft Command	12/46	34103	Calstock	1/50
34050	Royal Observer Corps	12/46	34104	Bere Alston	4/50
34051	Winston Churchill	12/46	34105	Swanage	2/50
34052	Lord Dowding	12/46	34106	Lydford	3/50
34053	Sir Keith Park	1/47	34107	Blandford	4/50
34054	Lord Beaverbrook	1/47	34108	Wincanton	4/50
34055	Fighter Pilot	2/47	34109	Sir Trafford Leigh Mallory	5/50
			34110	66 Squadron	1/51

*Originally named *Wells*.

APPENDIX C

CAB LAYOUTS OF THE BULLEID PACIFICS

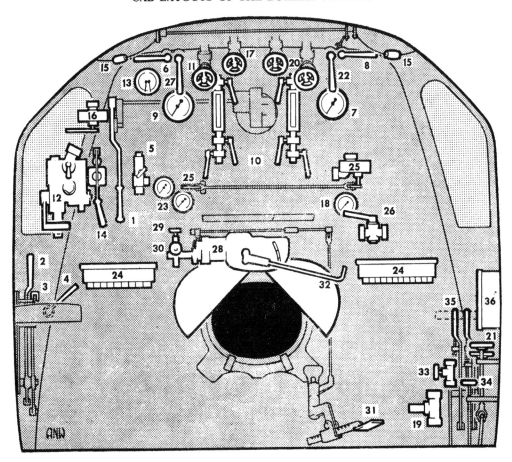

" MERCHANT NAVY " CLASS

1. Regulator handle.
2. Steam reversing gear control lever.
3.   ,,   ,,   ,, setting indicator.
4.   ,,   ,,   ,, clutch control.
5.   ,,   ,,   ,, lubricator.
6.   ,,   ,,   ,, steam supply valve.
7. Boiler steam pressure gauge.
8.   ,,   ,,   ,,   ,, cut-off valve.
9. Steam chest pressure gauge.
10. Water level gauges.
11. Ejector steam supply valve.
12. Ejector and vacuum brake control.
13. Duplex vacuum gauge.
14. Engine steam brake control.
15. Whistle cord hand grips.
16. Blower valve.
17. Steam heating supply valve.
18.   ,,   ,, pressure gauge.

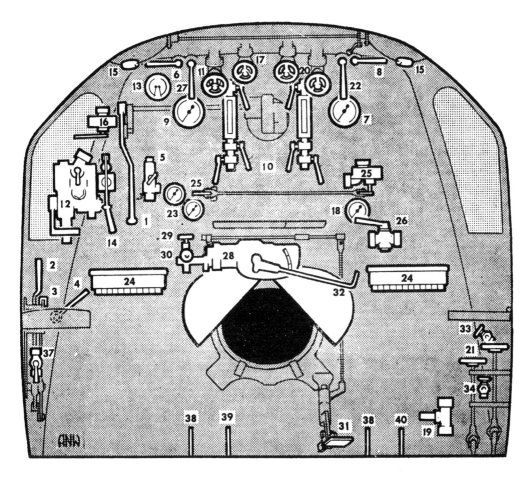

"WEST COUNTRY" CLASS

19. Steam heating pressure relief valve.
20. Live steam injectors' steam supply valves (2).
21. Steam and water cock controls for injectors (4 wheels).
22. Cylinder lubricating atomiser steam supply valve.
23. Lubricating oil pressure gauges.
24. Axle-box lubricating oil-boxes.
25. Steam sanding valve and driver's extension lever.
26. Electric lighting generator steam supply valve.
27. Steam operated firedoor steam supply valve.
28. Firedoor operating cylinder.
29.   ,,   ,,   ,,   inlet valve.
30.   ,,   ,,   ,,   drain cock.
31.   ,,   ,,   ,,   control pedal.
32. Firedoor manual operating lever.
33. Coal slacking hose water valve.
34. Tender spray valve.
35. Ash-pan damper controls. "Merchant Navy" diagram only.
36. Speed recorder, when fitted.
37. Windscreen water spray valve.   "West Country" diagram only.
38. Rocking grate controls (2).   ,,   ,,   ,,   ,,
39. Drop grate control.   ,,   ,,   ,,   ,,
40. Ash hopper doors control.   ,,   ,,   ,,   ,,

APPENDIX D

THE BULLEID PACIFICS—DIAGRAMS AND DIMENSIONS

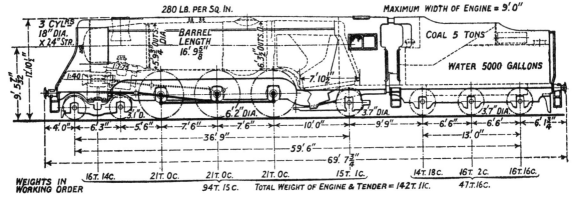

"MERCHANT NAVY" CLASS (Nos. 35001-10)

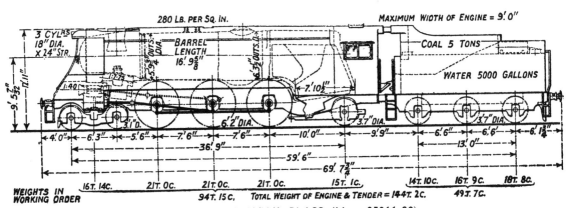

"MERCHANT NAVY" CLASS (Nos. 35011-30)

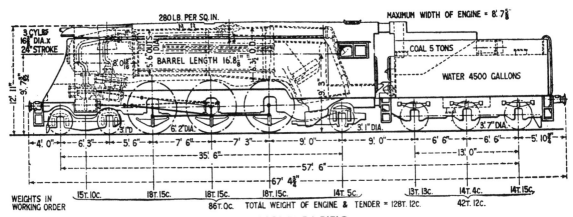

THE LIGHT PACIFIC

[Diagrams by courtesy of "The Railway Gazette"

80